MW00471164

REMARRIAGE IS ADULTERY
UNLESS . . .

Remarriage is Adultery
Unless . . .

**What the Bible says about divorce
and its outcome**

David Pawson

Anchor Recordings

Copyright © 2011, 2013 David Pawson

The right of David Pawson to be identified as author of this work
has been asserted by him in accordance with the
Copyright, Designs and Patents Act 1988.

First published in Great Britain 2011
Revised Edition 2013

Published by
Anchor Recordings Ltd
72 The Street, Kennington, Ashford TN24 9HS UK

All rights reserved.
No part of this publication may be reproduced or transmitted
in any form or by any means, electronic or mechanical,
including photocopy, recording or any information storage
and retrieval system, without prior permission
in writing from the publisher.

Cover design by Roger Judd

The publisher acknowledges with appreciation that text in the
Prologue to this work has been taken from
Once Saved, Always Saved? by David Pawson
Copyright © David Pawson 1996
Reproduced by permission of Hodder and Stoughton Limited

ISBN 978 0 9569376 9 8

Printed by CreateSpace

Contents

Prologue

I was travelling by train to London. The last halt to pick up passengers was at Clapham Junction. A man boarded my carriage at the far end, sat down, stared at me for some minutes before walking down the aisle and taking a seat facing me. As I recall, the conversation went like this:

'I think I recognise you. Are you a preacher?'

'Yes. Where would you have seen me?'

'Fifteen years ago, someone brought me to Guildford to hear a preacher and I think it was you.'

'It almost certainly was. Are you a Christian?'

'Yes. [pause] Can I ask you something?'

'I can't guarantee an answer, but what's the question?'

'Well, it's like this – I've left my wife and I'm now living with another woman.'

'Why did you leave your wife?'

'Because I met this other woman and fell in love with her.'

'So what do you want to know?'

'If I get properly divorced and marry this other woman would that put it right in God's sight?'

'No, I'm afraid it wouldn't.'

'Then what would?'

'Leaving this woman and returning to your wife.'

'I thought you'd say that.'

'I believe it's what Jesus would say if you asked him.'

This produced a silence between us. By now the train was slowing down for Waterloo and I realised I probably only had a minute or two more with him. I wanted to kindle that fear of the Lord that is the beginning of wisdom, so I reopened the conversation with:

'You have a difficult choice to make.'

'What's that, then?'

'You can either live with this woman for the rest of this life or with Jesus for all the next, but you can't do both.'

His eyes filled with tears but he jumped on to the platform and disappeared among the crowd. I felt a little of what Jesus must have felt when the rich young ruler left him. I prayed he would never be able to forget what I had told him until he had repented.

But was I right to say what I did? Was I telling him the truth or trying to frighten him with a lie? What he really wanted was an assurance that his sin would not affect his salvation. This I could not give him.

The same issue had arisen a month or two earlier, this time not with one person but with many thousands. I was the main speaker at the evening sessions of Spring Harvest at Minehead and given the task of expounding Paul's letter to the Philippians. I reached verse 11 of chapter 3 ('and so, somehow, to attain to the resurrection from the dead') and pointed out that even Paul himself did not take his future salvation for granted, but feared being 'disqualified' himself (1 Corinthians 9:27). I backed this up with texts from every part of the New Testament. I then spoke of those who 'play games with God because they are sure they have a ticket to heaven', citing as an example Christians who leave their marriage partner for someone else, whether they just 'live' with the new person or go through divorce and remarriage. Many such still go to church, claim God is blessing their new relationship and expect to go to heaven. But sin is still sin, whether it is in believers or unbelievers. God has no favourites. We are justified by faith, but we shall be judged by works.

These brief statements nearly caused a riot! One of the platform party leapt to his feet at the end of my address and repeatedly shouted: 'Nothing can separate us from the love of God in Christ Jesus', calling on the musicians to lead us all in a chorus based on that verse.

Then one of the main sponsors led in prayer for me and my poor wife 'because David doesn't always get things right'. The situation was saved by Roger Forster, who took the microphone and said we should be thinking about the message, not the messenger. He made an appeal, to which there was a massive response, led by seven men in tears. There were not enough counsellors to cope and the one in charge told me later that they had never seen such real repentance in the counselling room.

The tape of my talk was banned from circulation, later released after many protests – but only after an 'explanatory comment' had been added to the effect that I had been unable to qualify my remarks due to shortage of time – which was simply not true.

Thus ended my career at Spring Harvest. The 'double whammy' of questioning 'once saved, always saved' and accusing Christians who deserted their spouses for another of living in sin proved too much. I came away with the urge to write two books dealing with these vital issues of belief and behaviour.

The first was *Once Saved, Always Saved?*, published by Hodder and Stoughton in 1996 (the Prologue so far has been taken from it, with permission). Now, fifteen years later, here is the second. It has been the more difficult to write, hence the delay. There have been many other books on the same subject, published on both sides of the Atlantic. I have read most of them, contacted some of their authors and had edifying discussions with others. But the major delay has been due not to this research but the search for my own convictions. I need hardly add that the view here presented is my own and no-one else's. Nor is it final, but hopefully it will help readers to reach their own conclusions.

One final comment. Those who express reservations on this subject have been accused of being harsh and cruel at worst, hard and unfeeling at best. If their own marriage is stable they are told they cannot understand the trauma of a failed one. Sadly, I can assure readers that our family is one of that increasing number who have had to face the pain, indeed agony, of broken marriages among close relatives and friends. Writing this book can only add to the emotional cost, but my concern over the deteriorating standards within the Church must override even that.

1

WHAT GOD SAID

Sex was God's idea. It was therefore a 'good' idea. But it was also a powerful one, which would be a major factor influencing human relationships.

It is hardly surprising that the Bible has so much information about the use and abuse of this physical and emotional force, from one end to the other, from Genesis to Revelation. All God's gifts can be used to help or hurt ourselves and each other. It would be astonishing if the good Lord had not instructed us how to handle them. The purpose of this volume is to explore those instructions.

We begin where the Bible begins, with the creation of outer space, planet earth and everything in it. Significantly, it is the result of ten commandments ('let there be') from the throne of heaven, executed by the Spirit of God on earth.

Though plants and animals were previously capable of reproduction, most of it sexual, division of the human race into two genders is set in the context of bearing a unique divine image, separately as male and female and together as two persons in one.

We must pause to consider how and when the story of creation was released. It stands on its own in its poetic and mathematical character (see chapter 2 in my compendium *Unlocking the Bible*, HarperCollins, 2003). Yet it does not seem to have been known about before the time of Moses. For example, neither Adam nor Abraham observed the Sabbath. Since no-one was present to observe the beginnings it would have to have been a divine revelation at some later point and hints suggest Moses was the recipient.

However, the style of narrative changes with the introduction of geography and history (from Genesis 2:4) and human memory begins to play a part in the account, a more efficient faculty in days before writing. The entire perspective switches from the celestial to the terrestrial. Whereas the creation of sex is in the former context, the first instructions about it are in the latter (2:24-25).

They come in the context of Eve's cloning to be a fit helper for Adam. She is 'made' after, from and for him; all three points are taken up in the New Testament, as is his authority in naming her. Then come the implications for the relationship between the two of them, defining marriage for the rest of time.

First, it is a *heterosexual* relationship, between male and female.

Second, it is a *monogamous* relationship, between 'a man' and 'his wife', between one male and one female. Polygamy was never in God's mind.

Third, it is a *permanent* relationship. With Adam and Eve it would have been eternal had not their sin introduced death, but even then it was 'till death us do part'. Coming together involves a permanent 'leaving' one family (for Adam's sons onward) and 'cleaving' to form another. The latter notion is akin to being 'glued'; putting it crudely, husband and wife are 'stuck' with each other!

Fourth, it is a *combined* relationship. The two become 'one flesh'. This is much more than connected bodies. The couple are an entity. In some way more profound than physical they have been joined in a bond for life.

These two verses are crucial to the rest of scripture. Both Jesus and Paul quote them verbatim as the primary source for their teaching on sexual matters, as we shall see.

Before leaving them, we must note that it is a mistake to refer to this as God's 'ideal', a word which implies a target to be aimed at rather than a standard expected to be achieved. 'Intention' is a better word, suggesting the pattern laid down for all.

We are including in this chapter a reference to what have become known as 'The Ten Commandments'. We have already hinted that they may have been revealed to the same person who was given the story of creation, Moses, and therefore about the same time. Furthermore, they were written down by God himself, with his own finger (Exodus 31:18; cf. John 8:6). This is just one way in which the 'Ten Words' are distinguished from the rest of the Mosaic legislation (see chapter 2).

The thread running through all ten is respect. Respect for God's uniqueness, name and day. Respect for one's parents and other people's lives, marriages, property and reputation. The tenth alone deals with inward motivation rather than outward behaviour.

We are concerned with the seventh, which declares

marriage sacrosanct. Sexual intercourse is strictly limited to one's spouse. There is no direct reference here to premarital promiscuity; that is dealt with elsewhere. But there is an absolute prohibition of extra-marital misbehaviour as one of the fundamental acts of rebellion against the Creator and Redeemer of Israel (v. 2). This brings up the question whether God intended a wider application of these basic laws than to the people he rescued from slavery in Egypt and the nation they founded.

On the basis of conformity between the covenant peoples of the old and new covenants, Israel and the Church, there is a widespread assumption that they apply to both. They have been used in Catechisms and adorned many ecclesiastical interiors to undergird Christian ethics. Certainly most of them are alluded to in the New Testament.

The exception seems to be the fourth, concerning Sabbath observance (e.g. Romans 14:5-8; Colossians 2:16-17). However, the seventh is clearly carried through.

Many believe they were intended to be a foundation for all civic legislation as well. King Alfred made them the basis for English law, which ultimately influenced the 'Judaeo-Christian' culture of Western society, making murder, adultery, theft and false testimony crimes as well as sins. It was not so easy to do this with the tenth!

Whatever, it is clear that he who invented sex has surrounded its exercise with simple but severe restrictions, which may be summarised as absolute chastity outside marriage and absolute fidelity inside.

2

WHAT MOSES SAID

It may seem strange to consider the Mosaic laws in a different chapter to the Ten Commandments, so associated with his name. But there are clear distinctions between them and this is one way to draw attention to them.

We have already pointed out that God wrote down the ten and Moses wrote down the six hundred and three others, the former at the top of Mount Sinai, the latter at its foot and elsewhere on the journey to the promised land of Canaan. We may say that God gave the ten to Moses and the rest *through* him, though all were directed to the same people.

We could say that Moses is primarily concerned with the interpretation and application of the basic ten principles and particularly the final six, though he does introduce much new material. But the main difference lies in the way the laws are expressed. There is a clear trend from the 'apodeictic' to the 'casuistic' style, to give them their technical titles. That is, from the categorical: 'You shall not . . .' to the conditional: 'If you do . . . then . . . .' There is a shift from absolute prohibitions to relative regulations, a consideration of circumstances. This involves going into much more detail.

A further point to notice is the holistic nature of 'the law', or 'the Torah' (= instruction) as it is called in Hebrew. It covers the whole of life: food, clothes, marriage, war, etc. Furthermore, there is no division between 'sacred' and 'secular' aspects of life. Ceremonial, civil and moral laws are integrated into one legal system. That is why to break any of it is to break the whole of it (Deuteronomy 27:26; cf. Matthew 5:19; Galatians 3:10; James 2:10). The Western mind wants to classify them and treat them separately.

Whereas the ten were clearly directed to the individual '*you* shall/shall not . . .', the Mosaic laws clearly have a corporate bent. The social life of the people is constantly in mind, as is the community's responsibility to administer punishment for infringement. The objective is clearly to present a holy, healthy and therefore happy society to a world failing to achieve it.

Various sanctions are to be applied. The one retribution not mentioned is imprisonment.

With these preliminary observations in mind, we turn to three passages which have been quoted in connection with the debate on divorce and remarriage. Rather than take space to reproduce these in full, the reader is requested to have an open Bible alongside and read the appropriate text *before* reading the comments here.

Exodus 21:7-11 (read)

The context is female slavery, the sale of a daughter to be a wife. If her husband is not satisfied with her, he cannot sell her on the open market, where she might be purchased by a foreigner (as Joseph was). But she could be 'redeemed', bought for a price, by a fellow-countryman. Or she could be passed on to a son to be his wife, but in this case she must be given the full rights of a daughter. A third possibility is to keep her on and marry another woman as well (Moses did not ban bigamy). In this case the first must still have her needs of food, clothing and sex fully supplied. If not, she has the right to go free, without any payment.

It is this last point that has recently been picked up in a Christian treatise on divorce. The argument goes like this: if a slave wife could go free if her needs for food, clothes and sex were not met, surely any wife today, including a Christian wife, could claim the same. If this is a sound deduction, then a number of valid 'exceptions' have been added to the single one of Jesus. In a word, neglect can set one free *from* a marriage and *for* another.

Deuteronomy 22:13-30

This is not often referred to in debates on divorce, but we shall see (in chapter 5) how relevant it is, though its primary reference is to premarital promiscuity.

In Israelite culture a bridegroom expected his bride to be a virgin. He did not expect to pay for second-hand goods. The penalty for discovering he had been 'cheated' in this way was very severe, she was stoned to death. But such 'rough justice' needed to be protected from abuse.

A false accusation could be used as an excuse for a quick escape from a regretted partnership. It was the duty of the bride's father to protect his daughter's reputation and her life, by reporting the situation to the civic authorities and producing evidence of her virginity (bloody bedsheets after a ruptured hymen). Punishment for the lying bridegroom was to pay substantial compensation to the bride's father and remain married to the girl as long as she lived. He could have divorced her simply because he 'disliked' her (see Deuteronomy 24 in next section) but now he never can.

The next case dealt with is adultery, where a man has intercourse with another man's wife. When discovered ('found') *both* must die and both *must* die. There can be no forgiveness by the 'innocent' husband (contrast John 8:3-4).

The following situation gives a vital insight into Jewish culture. Note that 'a virgin pledged to be married' is *already* a 'man's wife' and sex with her constitutes adultery. Betrothal then was taken far more seriously than engagement is now and a separation before the relationship had been consummated was a 'divorce' (cf. the situation of Joseph and Mary; Matthew 1:18-19). Such an 'adultery' also demanded the death of both involved.

Of course it all depended on whether the premarital sex was consensual or forced. If it happened in the cramped conditions of a town and the woman had not cried for help, which would easily have been heard and quickly responded to, it was assumed that she had voluntarily co-operated. If it had happened out in the country, where cries would not have been heard, she would be given the benefit of the doubt and assumed to have been forcibly raped.

Had she not even been engaged to be married, the death penalty was not imposed on either. However, if they were discovered, they had to be married and the groom pay the bride's father an appropriate sum.

The passage closes with one forbidden marriage of 'consanguinity', namely a man and his father's wife (who may or may not have been his actual mother; see 1 Corinthians 5:1).

The main points to note in all this are that most premarital sex carries the death penalty and if one of the parties is engaged it constitutes adultery.

Deuteronomy 24:1-4 (read)

Unlike the previous passage studied, this one is always brought up in debate, primarily because it is the only direct mention of divorce and remarriage in the Mosaic body of legislation.

It is important to notice what it does *not* say on the subject. It neither commands nor prohibits divorce. It simply accepts that men will divorce their wives and marry others. It does mention the usual method of giving her a certificate (whether this states the reason for it we are not told, but with it she has proof that she is free to marry again) and sends her out of his residence. That is all that is required. Note that in the case cited she does find a second husband, who also dismisses her in similar fashion.

All that is forbidden is a third marriage to her first husband. She cannot go back to him but must find someone else. To go back to the original would be offensive to God and in some way pollute the whole country (we can only speculate exactly how but must take God's word for it).

And that's all! It is quite astonishing that discussion of the application of this passage should focus as it has on the grounds for divorce. The attention is not on this issue and was probably not in Moses' mind at all. Nor is there any hint that Moses would have limited divorce to the reasons mentioned.

The reason given for the first divorce has been highlighted. It is an obscure phrase, not easy to translate. It has a certain offensive tone – indecent, unclean, naked – and might refer to some blemish or even deformity only visible to the husband after the marriage. But nobody really knows and it does not really matter. The one thing we can say for sure is that it does not refer to adultery, for which the only action that could be taken was death, not divorce. What makes the discussion superfluous is that her second divorce, equally accepted, was for no other reason than her husband's 'dislike' of her. And we have no idea why he didn't like her.

We could leave it there, but later Jewish scribes were not content to do so. As we shall see (in chapter 4), they used this text in a way that was never intended, to debate the legitimate grounds for divorce, even with Jesus himself. Christians have followed suit, especially those who believe these laws apply to the Church as well as Israel, an assumption we must look at before we close this chapter. Meanwhile, we can summarise this section by stating that there was only one situation in which Moses banned remarriage after divorce: to a former husband.

Note that there is no mention of a wife divorcing her husband. The possibility was not considered.

* * * * *

In closing, we need to raise two general issues. The first is the significance of such regulation of social practices. The second is how far regulations in the 'old' covenant are binding on those in the 'new'.

Social evils or simply practices with harmful effects need to be controlled in any society, if only to restrict their influence. But legal provisions for their constraint in no way sanction their legitimacy. For example, the licensing of brothels or casinos in no way endorses the social benefits of prostitution or gambling. It is a way of controlling, even restricting, such habits. It is a recognition that fallen human nature will want to do these things anyway and it is the lesser evil to have some public control than none at all. This is an argument which has been advanced by some campaigners for abortions under professional rather than amateur backstreet hands. But all such legislation runs the risk of the naïve assumption that 'if it's legal it must be alright'.

Of necessity, such social legislation must involve moral compromise. But acceptance does not mean approval. Moses 'accepted' such things as slavery and polygamy which were part of the social fabric of his day and therefore issued laws for their control but in no way implied divine favour. This is particularly true of his treatment of divorce. We shall see that Jesus himself drew a distinction between God's intention and Moses' concession to human weakness (Mark 10:5). We must be careful to do the same.

This brings us to the other question, the Christian use of Moses' laws. How binding are they on disciples of

Jesus? Opinion varies between total relevance to none at all, depending in turn on whether the relationship between Israel and the Church is one of continuity or discontinuity. Behind that is the fundamental issue of how the 'Old' Testament relates to the 'New'. The very names of the two parts of our Bible contain a wrong answer, since 'testament' and 'covenant' are synonyms, suggesting there are only two covenants in scripture. There are at least five major ones: Noahic, Abrahamic, Mosaic, Davidic and Messianic. All five are mentioned in both Testaments. Only one is called 'old' (the Mosaic) and has been replaced by the only one called 'new' (the Messianic).

This is why the Mosaic covenant established at Mount Sinai is regarded in the New Testament as temporary (Galatians 3:17-25) and obsolete (Hebrews 8:7-13). Logically, this means that the Mosaic legislation is also past its sell-by date. But Christians are not always logical!

Most have taken the ten commandments very seriously indeed, including them in Catechisms and Communion services, inscribing them on church walls. Yet they have paid scant attention to the six hundred plus bye-laws added by Moses.

Few, if any, would advocate a return to the punishments he advocated. Over a dozen sins deserved capital punishment, including a son's rebellious attitude. Exact physical retribution (eye for eye, tooth for tooth, hand for hand, burn for burn, wound for wound, bruise for bruise: Exodus 21:24) was demanded for serious injury. Even a woman's hand could be cut off if she had grabbed an opponent's genitals during a fight with her husband.

Many requirements are totally ignored, from wearing clothes of unmixed material to twelve months' honeymoon leave for soldiers. Bearing in mind that Moses demanded that everybody promised to keep all the laws all the time, it is amazing that anyone would undertake such a commitment, though the Israelites did (Exodus 19:8). But the New Testament contains no such vows relating to Moses' laws. Indeed, Paul's militant objection to circumcising his Gentile converts was that it would obligate them to 'keep the whole law' (Galatians 5:3). He argued that Christians were as 'dead' to 'the law' as Christ himself was after his crucifixion (Romans 7:1-6, a passage we shall look at again).

It therefore seems inconsistent, if not hypocritical, for Christians to use 'the law' in a selective manner, quoting some of its requirements but not others. This is especially so when seeking to establish a biblical case for a viewpoint, for example, against homosexual activity. The most that can be established in that way is that God disapproved of it in Israel; but there is ample evidence for the wider application in the New Testament. And this is the test. Any Mosaic legislation upheld by Jesus or the apostles is still applicable. It has become part of the 'law of Christ'.

The law of Moses concerning divorce is only relevant to a Christian discussion insofar as it illuminates the Jewish background against which the Pharisees challenged Jesus to reveal his stance. Christians are not 'under the (that) law'.

3

WHAT PROPHETS SAID

Israel was a wife and God (Yahweh) was her husband. This was the basic insight underlying much of what the prophets said. They saw the covenant made with the fledgling nation at Sinai as analogous to a wedding, with vows made on both sides. For a vivid metaphorical description of the relationship from the birth of the nation to her courtship, read Ezekiel 16:1-14. Jews have seen the Song of Solomon as an analogy, even pressed it as an allegory, of their kinship with the Almighty.

It gave God's spokesman a ready simile when the very first of the ten commandments was broken and Israel, 'went after' other gods. She became an unfaithful wife, even a 'prostitute', above all an adulteress (see Ezekiel 16:15-34 for a searing indictment). What would this do to the marriage and what would that mean for human marriages? We look at three of the prophets and their message.

Hosea 1-3
The prophets were often called to demonstrate the 'word of the Lord' in their lives as well as declare it with their lips. Jeremiah had to remain single and would die young. Ezekiel would lose his wife but must not mourn for her.

Hosea had perhaps the hardest lot. He was to marry a woman of doubtful morals and reputation. He would become the father of three children, not all of whom would be his. Then she would leave and go back on the streets from which he had taken her. But he was not to leave her there but go and search for her, rescue her from her pimp, bring her home again, discipline her, then resume conjugal relations. Having done all this, he would be in a position to share convincingly how God felt about his people.

He was the last prophet to be sent to the ten northern tribes of 'Israel', after they had broken away from 'Judah' in the south and before they were invaded and deported by Assyria. He followed Amos, with his message of justice and judgement. Significantly, Hosea's final appeal for repentance focussed on mercy. It was a *cri de coeur* of unrequited love (11:1) but it fell on deaf ears.

However, in Hosea's own experience there was clearly a hope of recovery. The 'hound of heaven' would hunt his people again. The marriage could and would be restored. This suggests that, called to be holy as he is holy, God's people should also hold open the door to reconciliation when their partners are unfaithful.

Jeremiah 3:1-10
At first sight this prophet seems to take the very opposite line to Hosea. The ten tribes of 'Israel' in the north have by now disappeared into captivity. And the Lord says he has given them a certificate of divorce and sent them away! This sounds like a final dissolution of any marriage between them.

Believe it or not, Christians have used this to justify their own divorces. 'If God can do it, so can we.' Before jumping to this conclusion we need to look more carefully into the passage and its context.

Attention is now focussed on the remaining two tribes in the south, Judah and Benjamin (together they took the collective name of the larger, Judah, from which would come the word 'Jew'). They had seen what happened to her sister 'Israel', banished for her 'adulterous' behaviour, yet Judah was now just as bad, if not worse, just as unafraid of God's judgement and therefore facing the same fate: divorce.

But the metaphor begins to break down when the context is examined. It is not exactly parallel to the breakdown of a human marriage. The passage opens with a reference to the Mosaic regulations in Deuteronomy 24 we have already looked at, pointing out that it would defile the land if a woman returned to her husband after having been with other men. Humanly speaking, it would have been very wrong for God to take either sister, Israel or Judah, back into a 'covenant' relationship they had both betrayed.

However, God is God. He can act above and beyond laws made for human behaviour. He would have taken Israel back had she 'returned', i.e. responded to Hosea's verbal and visual appeal. God even says he 'thought' she would, but she didn't (verse 7; we won't discuss the implications of such a remark for his foreknowledge!)

The section following (3:11-4:1) gives ample proof, with its repeated plea 'return', that he hoped Judah would change her mind and repent before it was too late. But she was as stubborn and rebellious as her sister and was also 'sent away' to Babylon.

End of story – or it would have been in any other 'divorce'. The history of God's people Israel would have ended here. But it didn't. God is God and often does the unexpected. Before he finished his ministry, Jeremiah had promised that the Lord would bring them back from exile. 'For I know the plans I have for you,' declares the Lord, 'plans to prosper you and not harm you, plans to give you hope and a future' (29:11). God may have removed the Jews from their land but he had never rejected them (Romans 11:1). They may break their marriage vows to him but he will never break his to them (Leviticus 26:44; Jeremiah 30:11; Ezekiel 16:60 and many other references). His certificate of divorce is temporary. His 'new' covenant will be for Israel and Judah (31:31).

Malachi 2:13-16

By this time the children of Israel had returned from exile in Babylon, though by no means all of them. Having spent a lifetime there, many were unwilling to leave their social and commercial security to face the rigours of rebuilding a nation from its ruined capital, Jerusalem. Their leaders, Ezra and Nehemiah, were also concerned about a moral and spiritual recovery. Among other lapses from God's standards was an increase in mixed marriages, with spouses from outside the chosen people, expressly forbidden in Moses' Torah. Ezra confessed it with shame (see chapter 9 in his book) while Nehemiah dealt with it quite drastically (see chapter 13 in his book), pulling out the men's hair and demanding that the practice stop immediately. But it had continued.

Malachi was the last prophet sent by God until John the Baptist a few hundred years later. Far from recovering anything like the high spiritual state under king David, the nation was in serious decline. Slipshod habits of belief and behaviour were eroding the national religion, morality and general prosperity. The prophet confronted specific slackness in priests and people – from offering crippled and diseased animals for sacrifice to a failure to bring all the tithes. Among other changes were two connected with marriage.

As we have already mentioned, mixed marriage with non-Jews was still happening. Malachi went much further than Nehemiah's 'scalping' by calling down on the men divine excommunication from the chosen people (2:12).

But another evil was now rearing its head, destroying family life. Divorce was rapidly increasing. The Lord had been present as a witness to the commitment young couples had made to each other. He calls this a 'covenant', like those he himself had made with Israel. Just as those who married Gentiles were 'breaking faith' with his covenant (2:10-11), men divorcing the wives 'of their youth' (clearly they had grown tired of them) were 'breaking faith' with them. It was treachery, a betrayal.

Significantly, he appeals beyond Moses to God's original intention and action (in Genesis 2:24), as later Jesus himself would do. Note that he adds that the two have been one 'in spirit' as well as in flesh. Sexual intercourse in humans is more than physical coupling. It is the spirit that needs guarding to avoid marriage break-up.

'I hate divorce,' says the Lord. This is his last word on the subject in the Old Testament. It is a very strong statement, an emotional as well as a rational expression of abhorrence. Such action is utterly contrary to a covenant-keeping God. This is immediately followed by his hatred of 'a man's violence', which may refer to the physical and mental abuse which can precede a divorce. It is all followed by another warning to guard one's spirit against breaking faith.

Finally, notice that God is concerned about the children in such situations. They are less likely to be 'godly' if their parents divorce.

4

WHAT SCRIBES SAID

It is not easy to realise that one blank page between the Old and New Testaments represents a gap of a few hundred years. Jewish books were written during this period but there is a noticeable absence of a phrase that occurs nearly four thousand times in the Jewish 'scriptures', namely: Thus says the LORD (which in capitals signifies 'Yahweh', the name of God in Hebrew). They are to be found in some Bibles, notably Roman Catholic editions, under the title: 'Apocrypha', meaning 'hidden'.

During the endless interim they had no fresh revelation. There was 'no vision' (Proverbs 29:18). They were driven back to meditate on the past words of God, what he had already said to them. The records would be combined into a 'canon' (rule) of scripture by 100 B.C.

A new class of men arose in Israel called 'scribes' because they copied, by handwriting, these documents for use among the people. But they also began to 'explain' them, what they meant and how they should be applied to life. It was the beginning of what we now call 'rabbinic Judaism', which seems to give more attention and even authority to the expositions and applications than the text itself, especially when these were gathered together in such documents as the Mishnah and the Talmud. Scripture, or at least the first five books of it, was called 'the Torah' or the 'Pentateuch', but it was the 'traditions' that were studied in the 'yeshiva' (seminaries for training rabbis).

Inevitably, opinions differed. Rabbinic 'schools' of thought developed in matters of doctrine and ethics, belief and behaviour. Some were more conservative in outlook, others more liberal. Groups became associated with the names of their leading scholars. Their views filtered down to the ordinary folk through their local rabbis and were hotly debated, especially when daily life was affected. Ostensibly, it was a discussion of 'the law' of Moses but actually it was a debate about the 'traditions of the elders' (we shall note in the next chapter that Jesus did not challenge what 'you have read' but what 'you have heard it said').

Divorce, and therefore remarriage afterwards, was high on the list of topics for public disputation. It was rife in Greek and Roman society and increasingly common among the Jews, even in some of the most religious groups, like the Pharisees, who were among the keenest to debate its valid grounds.

There was general agreement among the protagonists. All seemed to agree that divorce was permissible and set both parties free to marry someone else. Typically, they only considered divorce as the husband's privilege, not the wife's; at any rate, he could do it without any application to a public court but she couldn't.

One other trend needs to be noted. The death penalty for adultery had been replaced by divorce, perhaps due to the Roman occupying power reserving the right of capital punishment for itself (though compare John 8:5 and Acts 7:58 with John 18:31). But it was still compulsory. An unfaithful wife *had* to be dismissed: she could not be forgiven.

So far there was general agreement, even to the point that there must be an adequate reason for the action. Here the consensus broke down. The debate centred on what were valid grounds and what were not. The issue focussed on two scholars, both claiming to interpret and apply correctly the Mosaic legislation in Deuteronomy 24.

SHAMMAI

This rabbi took a strict view, claiming that the one and only ground allowed by Moses was adultery by the wife. Such was the 'indecent' thing justifying her dismissal with a certificate. Nothing else was serious enough to dissolve the marriage. Needless to say, his was not the most popular opinion!

But we have already seen that this was one thing the Deuteronomic reason could not possibly have been. The compulsory penalty for adultery was death by stoning. This certainly set the husband free to remarry, as later divorce also would.

However, the claim that adultery justifies divorce can hardly appeal to Moses or the Torah. It is a 'tradition of men' (Mark 7:7-8).

HILLEL

This rabbi took a lax view, increasing the list of valid reasons to include many which today would be regarded as trivial, including burning the cooked food, flirting with other men and raising her voice in public. In other words, anything her husband found offensive. Obviously Hillel's position appealed to the husbands but not to the wives.

Hillel's school of thought was referred to as the 'any cause' attitude, since a husband could virtually find any fault he wanted with his spouse. When Jesus was asked for his opinion about divorce 'for every cause' (Matthew 19:3), he was surely being asked if he subscribed to Hillel's position.

Hillel and Shammai were contemporary with Jesus, which meant he would be drawn into the debate, as indeed he was. After Jesus' ministry was over, a third rabbi took the liberal side a final step further. His name was:

AKIBA (AQIBAH)

He came to the conclusion that a divorce needed no justification at all. A husband could simply send his wife away at will. That was his privilege as head of the house. If he had tired of her or met someone he liked better, that was nobody else's business. He could do what he wanted without being accountable to anyone. Carried *nem. con.* by one vote!

We mention this because there is a pattern here which has been seen in other societies, from strict limits through wider lists, to no restrictions at all. English legislation over divorce has followed the trend. It is a slippery slope.

It is time to turn from the Old Testament to the New. Since this volume is addressed to Christians, relevant passages will be examined at greater length and in greater detail.

5

WHAT JESUS SAID

This is the longest chapter in the book and has taken the most time to write. That is not just because in the whole Bible he said more on our subject than anyone else, it is because Jesus is the ultimate authority for all Christians. The one who called himself *the* way, *the* truth and *the* life surely deserves absolute trust and obedience. However, there are two anomalies (which basically means 'lawless') in contemporary Christianity, one general and the other specific, which seem to be diluting such a response.

The *general* one concerns our evangelism. Jesus told us to 'go and make disciples of all nations' (Matthew 28:19) and he defined a 'disciple' (which means a pupil, student or apprentice) as someone who has been 'baptised' (immersed in water) and is being taught to live by all that Jesus commanded.

Few evangelists do either of these two essentials. The very word 'disciple', the most common description of Jesus' followers in the New Testament, has been dropped in favour of 'Christian', which was at first a nickname used by unbelievers (Acts 11:26; 26:28) but was later adopted by believers (1 Peter 4:16). But 'Christian' has lost the undertones of learning and discipline. Getting decisions has replaced making disciples. A thirty second 'sinner's prayer' has replaced baptism.

The focus is on the beginning of the Christian 'Way' rather than the continuing journey. The need to live Jesus' way, a changed lifestyle, is hardly mentioned. Is this why repentance is less emphasised? It means to turn away from godless behaviour. The gospel calls people to repent and believe, in that order. John the baptiser expected 'fruit' of repentance (Luke 3:8) and Paul expected 'proof' (Acts 26:20), both in very practical ways. There has been a strange reversal – bring them to faith first and they can repent later. Can their sins be forgiven without repentance? Birth includes cutting the umbilical cord tying the baby to its previous existence in the dark.

There is a romantic version of becoming a Christian described as 'falling in love with Jesus'. Those holding this naïve notion need to be reminded that he said: 'If you love me, you will obey my commandments' (John 14:15). It is too easy to be sentimental, somewhat harder to be scriptural.

Evangelicals have a more subtle, theological reason for downplaying deeds of repentance. In their concern to preserve the truth of salvation by grace, they have developed an allergy to anything that smacks of human 'works'. Some even say that repentance and faith are the work of God in us, not something we have to do or are even able to do. Yet God commands us to do both. Trust and obedience together make up faith.

So, for a number of reasons, there seems to be less emphasis on conforming to Jesus' teaching as a major part of 'making disciples'. With static or declining numbers, many churches have a desperate desire to get more or even just keep what they have. User-friendly services don't major on Jesus' strict standards of behaviour or, like him, urge consideration of potential cost before embarking on a course they may later find too exacting. The gospel is both offer and demand.

Jesus had no inhibitions about spelling out in public the high standards of living required in the kingdom of God. Nor was he afraid of losing followers (Luke 9:51-62; John 6:66). Even his enemies acknowledged that 'we know that you speak and teach what is right, and that you do not show partiality but teach the way of God in accordance with the truth' (Luke 20:21). Pleasing God and pleasing people are mixed motives. To tell the truth, the whole truth and nothing but the truth is not a recipe for popularity.

The *specific* anomaly is the muted if not silent attitude to our Lord's teaching on divorce. He said nothing about abortion or homosexuality but Christians are unashamedly vocal on these issues. But he said a lot about remarriage after divorce and Christians are strangely quiet. There are now so many church members and ministers changing spouses, many preachers and teachers are reluctant to raise the issue for fear of disturbing and dividing congregations, even while 'blessing' remarriages solemnised outside church and holding 'divorce recovery' workshops which include remarriage as an option. Whereas once such would have been excommunicated, now it is those who question their 'rights' who are likely to be ostracised!

The trends we have outlined, both general and specific, underline the urgent need to go back to the scriptures, the four Gospels in particular, and make sure we really know and understand what Jesus said. One observation can be made quite quickly. His attitude to both divorce and remarriage was generally negative. Those who challenged him to declare his attitude publicly seem to have expected this.

It is unfortunate that any discussion of his teaching quickly homes in on 'exceptions', rather than making sure his 'rule' is first established. It then becomes an exercise in looking for loopholes. We shall begin by looking at his reservations and *why* he held them (the 'explanation' is in Luke and Mark). Only then will we consider any qualification (the 'exception' is in Matthew). Finally, we shall see how he dealt with situations himself (the 'example' is in John).

1. HIS EXPLANATION (Luke and Mark)

Luke 16:18 (read)

This is Jesus' shortest, simplest statement, so it is a good place to start. It is a categorical, unequivocal announcement without any qualification whatever. It does not criticise divorce itself as such, but certainly condemns remarriage afterwards, for both the divorcer and the divorcee. He is addressing the men, since the initiative, then and now, is usually theirs.

Before exploring the text, the context deserves attention. The statement is inserted, somewhat unexpectedly, in an altercation between Jesus and some Pharisees. The subject was money and Luke has placed the dialogue between two relevant parables, one about a man who valued people more than money and the other about a man who valued money more than people. After commending the 'unjust steward' for sacrificing possible gain in the present to ensure friends in the future, he recommends his hearers do the same but on a longer time scale, by using money to make friends after death rather than before (the second parable showed how using all one's money on things here leaves one with none hereafter).

Jesus added that it is impossible to devote one's whole life to making money and serving God; one or the other will take second place, usually God. The Pharisees openly ridiculed his logic. They regarded themselves as perfectly capable of pursuing financial and spiritual goals simultaneously. In a devastating indictment Jesus told them that they impressed men but not God, who detested them for their failure to recognise the significance of their own scriptures, the ministry of John the baptiser, or the incursion of the kingdom of heaven, which others were so eager and earnest about. Meanwhile they were preoccupied with the minutiae of Mosaic legislation, so occupied with the letter that they were missing the Spirit (assuming that v. 17 is sarcastic in tone).

It is then that Jesus throws in his comments on divorce. It is often those who succeed in commerce who trade in their wives for later 'models'. Wealth makes people dissatisfied with what they already have. This means that changing partners was a major habit in the life of rich Pharisees, who kept their consciences quiet by giving God a tenth of the herbs in their garden (Luke 11:42). They obviously thought it was alright to divorce and remarry but to Jesus it was all wrong. The important question is *why* he thought so.

In a word, it was sinning against God, breaking one of his laws. But which one is supremely significant. It was the seventh of the ten 'words' which God himself had written, the one forbidding adultery.

Few seem to realise the full implication of what Jesus was saying. Adultery is a sin committed by *married* people, when they engage in intercourse with anyone other than their spouse. This means that all those who have been divorced, however properly, are *still married in God's sight*. The relationship is still there. It has not been dissolved. They have not been set free to marry anyone else. The first 'covenant' still holds. It has been betrayed but not cancelled. Divorce may be recognised at the human level, but not at the divine. This cannot be said often or strongly enough, which is why we have said it in so many different ways.

The next thing to note is that Jesus did not limit the application of this startling statement to his followers, the Pharisees or even the Jews as a whole. It was a word for 'anyone' (literally, 'everyone') and for both parties, divorcer and divorcee, either of whom would be committing adultery on remarriage. Furthermore, the tense of the verb for 'committing adultery' is the present continuous, which means to go on doing something. Some have tried to say that only the initial act of remarriage and its first physical union is adultery, but Jesus is including all subsequent intercourse. To put it bluntly, remarriage after divorce is bigamy in God's sight. It is not a valid marriage.

One final point. Both the address and the content of Luke's Gospel indicate that he was writing for *Gentile* readers and one in particular, whose title hints that he may have been a judge or an advocate at Paul's trial in Rome. His second volume, which we call the book of Acts, appears to confirm this impression.

Before leaving this Gospel, there is another passage which has an indirect bearing on our subject:

Luke 20:27-35 (read)

This time we are dealing with another Jewish 'denomination' (which simply means a labelled group). If Pharisees were conservative in belief and behaviour, Sadducees were the liberal wing. The former believed in a general resurrection; the latter did not. They thought the idea bizarre.

Perhaps to discover which group Jesus would identify with, but more likely to ridicule his sympathy with the others, they proposed a conundrum for Jesus, based on the law that if a man died leaving a widow without a son his brother was honour bound to marry her and give her children, to preserve her name and property (Deuteronomy 25:5-6; it does not mention whether the brother was single or already married, so presumably polygamy was allowed in these circumstances).

When challenging Jesus' teaching as a rabbi, the Sadducees concocted a situation in which a wife lost seven husbands, all brothers, without producing a son and heir. Statistically improbable but theoretically possible! Since 'resurrection' meant the re-creation of the body rather than the immortality of the soul, the punchline question was which brother would have her as wife (i.e. sexual partner) then? I can imagine sly smiles between them as they waited for his answer. Gotcha!

It was swift in coming. Their question was based on the false assumption that marriages survived death, itself based on ignorance of divine power which was capable of creating different kinds of bodies, everlasting so not needing to reproduce or replace themselves, therefore like the asexual angels who were created and remain immortal.

Jesus then went on to challenge their cynicism by reminding them that the God of Abraham, Isaac and Jacob was God of the living, not the dead. The patriarchs were still very much alive, though no longer married.

The point of including this is to show that Jesus clearly believed that marriage will not survive beyond the grave and will never be revived as an exclusive bond between a man and a woman. In other words, the marriage bond is not indissoluble. Divorce does not dissolve it, but the death of one partner certainly does. Jesus did not challenge the assumption that after each husband's death the widow was free to marry again. He only challenged their assumption that marriages would be revised in the resurrection.

Summing up Luke's record of Jesus' teaching: remarriage is adultery unless . . . a spouse has died.

Mark 10:1-12 (read)

Here we find a much fuller account of Jesus' thinking, revealed in an argument between himself and some Pharisees. This time it is they who take the initiative and raise the subject. Mark makes it clear that their question was not from sincere enquirers. They were 'testing' him (the word is literally: 'tempting'), hoping that they could get him into trouble by what he said.

But with whom? The answer may lie in the geographical location of the discussion, which was on the *east* bank of the Jordan. They were in the territory of Herod Antipas, who had been responsible for the execution of John the baptiser, at the instigation of his wife Herodias, who bitterly resented John's public denunciation of their 'illegal' marriage. Were Jesus' antagonists hoping to cause a similar demise for him?

Or was it simply that whatever his viewpoint he would antagonise a substantial body of the public, whether that took the strict line of Shammai or the lax line of Hillel (which are described in chapter 4). Whatever, they were obviously setting a trap for him. But Jesus had some practice in escaping from such verbal hazards, with amazing wisdom.

The narrative is divided in two phases: first the public controversy with the Pharisees, then a private conversation with his disciples afterwards.

THE PUBLIC CONTROVERSY (verses 2-9)

The grounds for divorce were being hotly debated in Jesus' day, seemingly because its rate was increasing. But this was not what he was questioned about. They were asking whether he would accept *any* divorce at all as within the bounds of their law (i.e. the law of Moses, the Torah). A negative answer would have made him extremely unpopular with many, and a positive one would have thrown him into the arena of controversy.

Jesus answered their question to him with a question to them, a favourite technique of his (cf. Mark 11:28-30). His challenge was carefully worded. By 'Moses' he was referring to the first five books of the Bible, all attributed to his authorship, known to Jews as the 'Torah' and to Christians as the 'Pentateuch'. And he used the verb 'command', which means to order someone to do or not to do something. Of course, Moses never commanded anyone to divorce. The nearest he ever came to it was to forbid a divorced wife to remarry her first husband after divorce from a second. Nor had he defined valid grounds for divorce.

But Moses had 'permitted' it, the Pharisees argued, only to be told that it was a compromise, an accommodation with the 'hard hearts' of the people Moses had to deal with. This could refer to their stubborn rebellion against God ('stiff-necked') or, less probably, to their unforgiving irritation with each other. Whatever, its aim was to restrict their wilfulness. It was not the last word on the subject.

It was not the first word either. Jesus refers back to an earlier part of the Torah (Genesis 2:24), containing God's own original mandate for marriage, intended for universal application. As we have seen (in chapter 1), God's plan was heterosexual, monogamous and, above all, lifelong.

The God who made male and female (a reference to Genesis 1) has both the right and responsibility to order the relationship between them (as in Genesis 2). He reminds them that marriage is in some subtle way a union of two *persons* who have become 'one flesh'. Two into one will go! This has been an act of God, a supernatural intervention into every marriage, a miracle. To break up what he united is an act of human vandalism, destroying the Creator's handiwork. Jesus is not saying a marriage cannot be broken up but that it should not be. Not man cannot, but man must not. Matrimony is holy, sacred. To break it up is sacrilege.

It is worth pausing to ask why Jesus is talking like this. For him the day of compromise is over. No longer will laws, even for God's people, need to be lowered to cope with human weakness and wilfulness. A new day has dawned. God may have overlooked sins in the past 'but now he commands all people everywhere to repent' (Acts 17:30). God's moral standards are being lifted back up to 'normal'. Instead of laws being lowered to meet human nature, human nature will be lifted to meet divine standards. This is of the essence of the 'new' covenant, prophesied by Jeremiah (31:33-34) and Ezekiel (36:26-27) and which Jesus would establish through his death, resurrection and ascension. The 'old' covenant of Moses was 'becoming obsolete' (Hebrews 8:13). All this must have been in Jesus' mind as he responded to the Pharisees. His coming made their question irrelevant. Divorce should not even be discussed!

They may not have realised that he had really answered their question – by dismissing it! They could not read his mind or understand fully *why* he took such a radical approach, which virtually said no divorce at all. But he had not said this directly, so they may have been left wondering whether this is what he meant. The disciples of Jesus certainly were left in doubt.

THE PRIVATE CONVERSATION (verses 10-12)

Just as soon as they could get Jesus on his own, his inner circle of followers wanted him to clarify his position. Had they understood him correctly? Was he really dismissing all divorce and all remarriage afterwards?

This time Jesus gave a straight answer to a straight question. This was characteristic of his whole teaching method to the general public and especially his opponents, using obscure conundrums, parables which hid the truth from all but sincere seekers (Mark 4:9-13). But to those he had chosen to be his disciples (pupils) and eventually apostles (preachers) he explained things clearly and answered their questions directly. Which he did on this occasion, too.

His answer is almost identical with the one we have already looked at (in Luke 16:18). He gives the same basic reason for his 'no divorce' stance, that it does not dissolve the marriage, making a second marriage adulterous in God's sight. Again, it is the remarriage that is wrong. Notice, too, that it is a sin 'against her' (the first wife) as well as against God.

The only difference is that Luke is addressed to men only, who divorce their wives. Mark includes a word for wives who divorce their husbands, which was more typical of Greek and Roman society. Jesus' principles apply equally to them.

The other thing to be noticed is that this plain, clear statement was given only to the disciples in Mark but to the Pharisees themselves in Luke. The latter was much later, when Jesus was on his last journey to Jerusalem and ready to challenge his enemies more openly.

Finally, from considerable internal evidence and external tradition, biblical scholars are generally agreed that both Mark and Luke were primarily aimed at a *Gentile* readership, among whom divorce and remarriage were common. It is therefore significant that Jesus' teaching was given without qualification, without any 'exception'. The prohibition was absolute. When we turn to Matthew, the case is very different. Not all the early churches had all four Gospels, but we have and must take them all into account.

2. HIS EXCEPTION (Matthew)

Unlike Luke and Mark, Matthew contains two passages dealing with our subject (5:31-32 and 19:1-12), one of which is not to do with the Pharisees. However, the main difference is that both contain an 'except' clause, which qualifies the general rule in the other two 'Synoptic' (look-alike) Gospels.

Perhaps this is why most Christian discussions on divorce quickly home in on Matthew. Indeed, I have come across some who are not even aware of what Luke recorded. Is this because we are more motivated to find loopholes than to follow laws? Whatever, we seem more interested in what Matthew has to say. I don't believe that it is because it is the first Gospel in the New Testament or because it has more to say. It is because of that 'exception', which attracts our attention so quickly.

Before analysing the meaning of the *one* exception Jesus did make, we need to realise the huge significance of making *any* exception at all. It changes an absolute into a relative principle – from one which applies to all people in all situations to some people in some situations. It is no longer simple to apply; other factors must first be taken into account. A 'never' prohibition is changed into 'sometimes'. Luke and Mark were simple and straightforward. Matthew has made it far more complicated.

It is not easy to see how *any* exceptions are compatible with Jesus' appeal to Genesis 2. No exceptions are mentioned there and do not even seem to be contemplated at that stage. Jesus quoted from it apparently to rule out divorce altogether. Yet here in Matthew he is bringing it back into the picture.

Not surprisingly, some scholars have questioned the authenticity of the Matthaean record. Did Jesus really say there was an exception or do we owe this to Matthew himself, to reinforce his claim that even 'the smallest letter' and 'the least stroke of the pen' (the jot and tittle) will remain in force until 'everything is accomplished' (5:18), whatever that means? If so, did he add the exception unconsciously or was it deliberate? Or was it added by someone else, a copier of a very early manuscript?

There has been much speculation among those who are acutely aware of the problem we have exposed. It is not a question of contradiction but the addition created a strong tension between the absolute and relative versions.

This author is convinced Matthew's memory and his record were correct. Jesus did make an 'exception' to his 'rule'. There must be a reason why Matthew included it and, conversely, why Luke and Mark did not. I don't think the latter two had a lapse of memory. I believe the clue lies in their readership, i.e. who they were writing for. That may also point to the nature of the 'exception', as we shall see.

One difference is that Luke and Mark seem to be directed towards unbelievers, whereas Matthew is aimed at believers. He uses Mark for his basic structure but his unique feature is the collections of Jesus' teaching by this former collector of taxes. There are five such compendiums, all of them gathered around the theme of the kingdom of heaven, in chapters:

5-7:   The lifestyle of the kingdom.
10:     The mission of the kingdom.
13:     The growth of the kingdom.
18:     The community of the kingdom.
24-25: The future of the kingdom.

A quick reading of any of these 'sermons' quickly reveals their intended audience (look at 5:11-12; 10:16-18; 13:16-17; 18:18-19; 24:9-13). They are all addressed to those already in the kingdom, describing the duties and dangers of its citizens, its 'sons'.

Is that the clue we are seeking? It would leave unbelievers no excuse for divorce and believers with the 'privilege' of one good reason to do so. Is it likely that Jesus would offer his disciples a lower moral standard than the world? I think not! In every other sphere he called them to higher morality and promised them the help they would need to reach it.

Is there any other obvious difference between Matthew on the one hand and Luke/Mark on the other? Yes, there is. We have already noted that they were primarily addressed to Gentile (unbelievers), while Matthew is primarily, though by no means exclusively, for Jewish (believers). The evidence for saying this is as follows:

i. He begins with Jesus' genealogy, an unlikely approach to interest a Gentile reader! Here Jesus is immediately established as 'King of the Jews', by his descent from King David. And there is a coded message for Jews in Jesus' family tree. Like the Romans, Jews used letters instead of numbers (A=1, B=2, and so on) and gave names a numerical value, 'David' being 14. So Matthew has presented Jesus' genealogy in three phrases of 14 names each: Abraham to David, to the exile, then to Joseph.

This is all very interesting to Jews. The author recalls a Jewish man coming to faith in Jesus as his Messiah when he preached on Matthew 1:1-17.

By contrast Luke, writing for Gentiles, holds the genealogy back until the end of his third chapter and takes it back to Adam, not Abraham.

ii. He has far more links with the Jewish scriptures (what we call the 'Old Testament') than the other three Gospels. He alone quotes Jesus' protest that he had not come to abolish 'the law and the prophets' but to fulfil them. Matthew contains the strongest affirmations of Mosaic legislation (5:18-19, verses which perplex many Christians who believe they are not bound by it) and he delights to find prophetic prediction coming true in the life of Jesus (often introduced by the formula: 'that it might be fulfilled'; e.g. 2:6, 15, 17, 23).

Perhaps this is why Matthew has been put first in the New Testament, though it was not the first to be written; it is an excellent link with the Old, right next to Malachi in our Bibles.

iii. He uses the phrase 'kingdom of heaven' where the other Gospels use 'kingdom of God'. He is certainly not referring to a different kingdom, as some commentators have tried to prove. Identical texts prove that he has deliberately changed Jesus' own words. Why would he do that?

From the traumatic experience of the exile onwards, the Jews became hyper-sensitive to the danger of taking the name of the Lord in vain. They stopped using it, substituting euphemisms like 'heaven' instead (as in our phrase 'heaven help you'). To this day no-one knows how to pronounce God's name given to Moses and represented in Hebrew by the four consonants JHVH. It is certainly not 'Jehovah', more like 'Yahweh'. Even 'God' is printed as 'G-d' in newspapers.

Awareness of these scruples is the obvious explanation for Matthew's alteration if he had a Jewish readership in mind. He was avoiding unnecessary offence which might have prevented them from reading his 'good news'.

iv. He has gathered Jesus' teaching into five discourses, as we have already noted. Was this an unconscious or, more likely, conscious echo of the five books of Moses in the Jewish 'Torah'? Is he suggesting Jesus as the new lawgiver, the fulfilment of Moses' own prophecy (in Deuteronomy 18:15; cf. John 6:14; Acts 3:22-23)?

It is intriguing that the first and last 'sermons' were both given 'on the mount', reminiscent of Moses on Sinai.

v. He has changed Mark's teaching on divorce for both men and women who take the initiative to the men only custom in Jewish culture.

* * * * *

We have said enough to support Matthew's primary focus. Putting together the two major differences between

Matthew on one side and Luke and Mark on the other, we can say with some confidence that his Gospel was intended for Jewish believers. This would fit in with the tradition that it first surfaced in the occupied land of Israel itself, among the churches there. We often forget that the earliest Church was Jewish in membership and, indeed, was still regarded as a Jewish sect. Incidentally, a manuscript fragment of Matthew in the library of Magdalen College in Oxford shows it was written before the great division between church and synagogue, Christianity and Judaism, had taken place.

Readers may have become impatient with this lengthy diversion (distraction?) into the Jewish atmosphere of Matthew's Gospel, but if it explains why Jesus' 'exception' is only in that Gospel and not in Mark or Luke, it will have proved to be very important indeed. Bearing all this in mind, we can now examine the two relevant passages in detail.

Matthew 5:31-32 (read)
As part of the famous 'Sermon on the Mount', the first discourse on the Kingdom, here its lifestyle, the wider context is crucial to understanding.

Originally addressed to his disciples only, for which he took them away from where people lived (5:1), it was heard, in the end, by the general public who had followed (7:28). This change is reflected in its content; compare 5:13-16 with 7:13-14.

It begins with what kingdom citizens need to *be* rather than *do*, in order to be salt and light in the community, blessed and used by God. Their right lifestyle, their 'righteousness' must go well beyond the right outward actions demanded by the law and exemplified by the Pharisees. It must spring from the right *inward* attitudes, the pure heart. Jesus then draws a series of contrasts between what his audience has 'heard' from other teachers about the laws of Moses and what he 'says' about them. His first-hand authority ('but *I* say to you'), contrasted with their second-hand (the opinion of leading rabbis) will leave a deep impression (7:28-29).

His application of 'the law' to daily life is deeper, stricter and much harder to keep than traditional interpretations. Take the sixth, for example, 'You shall not kill' (Exodus 20:13, better translated, 'You shall not murder', since the penalty was capital punishment, which others had to 'execute'; Exodus 21:12). Jesus points out that actual murder is the end of a process which began in a heart full of anger or contempt. Since God sees the inside of a person, such feelings have already broken his law and deserved his judgement. There are far more murderers around than is generally realised. They just lack the means, the opportunity or the courage to do it. 'If looks could kill'!

The same is true of adultery. It begins inside, usually stimulated by what the New Testament calls 'the lust of the eyes' (1 John 2:16). To look at a woman and even think about going to bed with her is to have begun on a course of adultery, even though it never reaches the physical act. Few men can read this without a twinge of conscience. Fewer still have made the necessary resolution (Job 31:1).

But there is another surprising way of breaking the seventh commandment which Jesus went on to censure, the legal version as distinct from the physical and mental. This is the subject of our first passage in Matthew and the result of divorcing a partner.

It is in this connection that we have the first mention of an exception. However, before looking at that we need to ask what it is an exception *to*. In other words, we must first study the sentence in which an 'except' clause occurs, reading it without that qualification. The main verb is to 'make someone guilty of adultery', meaning someone else is responsible for the wrongdoing. In this case, it is the husband who has taken the initiative by divorcing his wife. By doing so he has *made* her an adulteress.

How has he done this? One possibility is that he has given her that reputation, since many could assume that that was the reason for his dismissal, remembering that the school of Shammai taught that adultery was the only valid ground. More likely, it is a reference to her almost certain remarriage. In a day when women could not apply for jobs and there was no social assistance for single women, her prime hope of support and security would be to find a second husband.

Jesus is totally consistent in denouncing remarriage after divorce as adultery. As we have seen, divorce does not dissolve the marriage bond, so it is a sin by a *married* person. Furthermore, the man who marries the divorced woman has also been made to commit adultery, since she is still married in God's sight. So the man who divorced his wife is directly responsible for setting a train of adultery in motion, causing others to break the seventh commandment, even though he has not (technically, in the letter) broken it himself. But God will hold him responsible for his wife and her second husband having done so.

Unless, that is, his wife was *already* guilty and dismissed for that very reason. But guilty of what? The problem is that Jesus does *not* use the word 'adultery' (in Greek: *moicheia*) at this point, about the divorce itself, but does use it immediately afterwards about the subsequent remarriage.

Jesus used another word as the original reason for the divorce, namely the Greek *porneia*, translated 'fornication' in the King James Bible. It is this that has caused endless debate and dissension. We ask for the reader's understanding if we postpone examination of its meaning until we encounter the word again in Matthew 19 where it is used in a context more relevant to our main theme.

For the moment it is sufficient to say that 'porneia' refers to behaviour that is both *sexual* and *sinful*. With this simple definition we can sum up what Jesus is saying here. He is primarily concerned with ways of breaking the seventh commandment. This can be done physically, mentally and legally. In the last case, by driving *others* (a divorced wife and her second husband) into an adulterous relationship, even without committing adultery oneself.

The only case in which the divorcing husband is *not* held responsible is where the wife was already engaged in sinful, sexual activity *before* the divorce took place. In that case the husband is not held responsible for her later immorality. She had already chosen that course. It is as simple as that.

Of course it is implied, though not specifically stated,

that the divorce was justified in the case of her infidelity, and therefore is permitted. In such circumstances a divorce *can* take place but there is not a hint that Jesus thought it *must*, as Jewish culture demanded. Indeed, as part of a sermon which contains so many exhortations to overlook insults and injustices, to turn the other cheek and go the second mile, to be reconciled before worshipping God, to forgive before expecting to be forgiven, to pray for enemies and bless those who make us suffer, Jesus would surely see divorce as the very last resort.

Turning to the other passage, we find a direct discussion of the reasons for divorce and again the 'exception' clause is included, though the wording is slightly different (from 'apart from' to 'not on'). We shall have to examine 'porneia' much more carefully in this context.

Matthew 19:1-12 (read)

The first thing to say is that this account is so similar to the one in Mark (10:1-12) that it must refer to the same occasion. It is in the same place, the east bank of the Jordan (Herod's territory), at the same time, on the last journey to Jerusalem, and with the same protagonists, the Pharisees. Indeed, the actual wording is such that many scholars believe that Matthew has copied Mark.

However, there are clear indications that he did not copy it slavishly, verbatim, but adapted it for his own purpose and readership. There are some real differences, even discrepancies, between the two accounts. The most obvious is that while both have the two phases, public controversy with the Pharisees followed by private conversation, the content of the second part is entirely different, though this can be regarded as complementary rather than contradictory.

In the public discussion, the mentions of Moses' legislation and Jesus' appeal to creation have been reversed, though this does not seriously affect the flow. In relation to Moses two verbs have been exchanged: the Pharisees use 'command' and Jesus uses 'permit'. Matthew omits 'against her' in his criticism of divorce, as he does all reference to wives divorcing husbands.

Perhaps the most significant difference is in the wording of the Pharisees' initial 'testing' question. In Mark they simply ask whether divorce is 'lawful'. That is, is *any* case covered by the Mosaic legislation? It is a general enquiry. In Matthew a phrase is added: 'for *every* cause'. This becomes a particular enquiry, for that phrase is probably a reference to the school of rabbi Hillel and his broader liberal view, as over against rabbi Shammai's narrow conservative view (for adultery only). In Matthew's version it seems as if they are trying to make Jesus declare which 'side' he is on in the current controversy and offend one party or the other with his reply. Indeed, if the 'exception' is taken to mean adultery, Jesus was exactly lining up with Shammai, though that would hardly explain the disciples' astonished reaction. But we are anticipating.

Apart from the exception, Matthew's account agrees in essence with Mark's, so all we said about that also applies here and does not need to be repeated. It is the major variations that must be carefully studied, namely the 'exception' and the conversation with the disciples.

First, then, the exception. We have already pointed out that Jesus did not use the word for adultery (Greek:

moicheia) in the phrase itself, though he does immediately afterwards, even in the same sentence. Had he done so, it would have saved a great deal of ink and hot air. Of course, Jesus did not speak in Greek, but we can assume that Matthew's choice of terminology reflected an original word in Hebrew or Aramaic which Jesus had used. So we will consider Matthew's use of *porneia* for the exception, what that would mean to him and his readers. It will simplify matters if we use the translation of the 'King James' Authorised version: fornication. There are three possibilities for the relationship between 'fornication' and 'adultery':

i. They have the *same* meaning and are interchangeable synonyms in this context. Imagine one circle with the letters 'F' and 'A' inside it.

ii. Their meanings *overlap* in some way, usually thought of as one including the other but not excluding other meanings. Imagine a smaller circle labelled 'A' inside a larger circle labelled 'F'.

iii. They have quite different meanings, which would be represented by two circles alongside each other, one with an 'F' and the other with an 'A'.

These three 'diagrams' cover all the main interpretations of the exception and we shall look at each in turn.

i. SAME MEANING

Most modern English translations have assumed or suggested this. The New International Version is typical, rendering it as 'marital unfaithfulness'. Many churches and Christians through the centuries have taken it this way. The change in terminology, from 'fornication' to 'adultery', is dismissed as having no theological significance, and thought of as being simply an example of literary variety probably owing more to Matthew's writing than Jesus' speaking.

This makes it much easier to apply in pastoral situations. Has adultery been committed or not? If it has, divorce and remarriage can be allowed and approved. If not, they cannot be.

However, this interpretation is open to abuse, in at least two ways. First, adultery can take place quite deliberately in order to be 'eligible' for a divorce. In the days when it was a legitimate ground in English law, it was a well known practice for Londoners to visit certain hotels in Brighton where staff could provide both a chambermaid for a night and written confirmation that they had been 'discovered' in bed together!

Second, where adultery has taken place *after* a marriage has broken up and the couple has separated and is *then* cited as justification for a divorce, it is surely an excuse rather than a reason.

These two evasions of reality were among the arguments used in the 1960s to change the law from existing grounds to one only: 'irretrievable breakdown of the marriage'. This also recognised the difficulty of proving either party to be totally guilty or innocent.

ii. OVERLAPPING MEANINGS

This usually takes the form of one larger circle including a smaller circle. 'Fornication' covers all examples of illicit sex, engaged in by the single and the married alike; whereas 'adultery' is only by the married.

This is probably the most widely accepted interpretation, mainly because 'fornication' (Greek *porneia*) appears to be applied to *both* single and married persons in the New Testament, particularly in the book of Revelation (2:21; 9:21; 14:8; 17:2, 4; 18:3; 19:2).

In addition to the anomalies mentioned above (in i. 'Same meaning'), this interpretation introduces more problems.

First, it introduces a wider range of grounds. Incest, paedophilia, homosexuality and even bestiality all qualify. If it includes reaching orgasm with anyone or anything other than one's spouse, could masturbation be squeezed into the list?

Second, since Jesus taught that mental adultery is as serious a sin as physical, what about pornographic magazines and films (on television) or even just a roving eye?

And what about spiritual 'adultery', such as Israel committed when 'going after other gods'? Does a partner changing religion justify divorce? Or even a believer becoming an unbeliever? We shall look at this situation again in 1 Corinthians 7:12.

It is fallen human nature to find loopholes in the law and then try to stretch them. Not surprisingly, those who take the wider meaning of 'fornication' press for the inclusion of other offences. They ask pointed questions like: why did Jesus only focus on sexual sin and hasn't the Church become obsessed with that as a result? Wouldn't he regard physical and mental cruelty as equally damaging to a marriage? And what about neglect, incompatibility, financial pressures and a host of other reasons for marriage breakdown?

Such imaginative speculation about what Jesus *might* have thought carries the danger of reading our own ideas into his mind and mouth. The inevitable conclusion is that he would approve most, if not all, divorces and remarriages. And some Christians are actually claiming this, in the name of his 'compassion', even or especially for guilty sinners. Surely adultery is not the unforgivable sin!

Accepting 'fornication' as equalling or including adultery *can* be the first step on a slippery slope, down which it is not easy to stop and draw a line, as many have found. This is an added reason for considering a third possibility:

iii. DIFFERENT MEANINGS

This assumes that Jesus himself quite deliberately chose to use different words, one (*porneia*) for the 'except' clause when speaking about divorce and the other (*moicheia*) when speaking about remarriage.

The basic scriptural reason for making a clear distinction between the two is that they are listed separately yet alongside each other in catalogues of sins and sinners, both by Jesus and the apostolic writers (see Matthew 15:19; Mark 7:21; 1 Corinthians 6:9; Hebrews 13:4). This makes an identical meaning impossible and an overlapping meaning unlikely.

What, then, distinguishes 'fornication' from 'adultery'? There must be some contrast between them. The simplest and most logical answer is that if one refers to illicit sex *after* marriage the other refers to illicit sex *before* marriage. This is certainly their definition in the English language. The Oxford Dictionary describes fornication as 'voluntary sexual intercourse between unmarried persons', and adultery as 'voluntary sexual intercourse of a married person other than with spouse' ('voluntary' distances both from rape). Does the English usage reflect the Greek, via the previous Latin version? It could well be.

Many may not realise how strong is the case for taking 'fornication' in this way, especially back in the time of Jesus. Consider the following arguments:

1. This explains why the 'exception' is only found in Matthew. We have already seen that this Gospel was primarily written for Jewish believers in the largely Jewish earliest churches. Jewish culture was a real factor to be taken into account, as it certainly was in the findings of the Jerusalem Council (Acts 15:28-29). Intriguingly, abstaining from fornication (the same word *porneia*) is one of the three things Gentile believers are exhorted to practise out of sensitivity to Jewish scruples, but surely that is incumbent on all believers anyway, Jewish or Gentile. However, Jewish culture was based on Mosaic legislation which required virginity in a bride, on penalty of death (Deuteronomy 22:20-21). This was 'proved' not to be the case either, most obviously, by becoming pregnant before the marriage or not bleeding when the marriage was consummated.

By the time of Jesus the punishment had been reduced from death to divorce, though both were compulsory. This is what nearly happened to Jesus' own parents, Joseph and Mary, also recorded in Matthew (1:19). Since betrothal was a binding commitment to marriage, to break it was considered equivalent to 'divorce'. Joseph, being a just (fair, righteous) man resolved to divorce her in a way that would minimise publicity and consequent disgrace. Like his namesake, he received divine revelation in dreams. Persuaded by the angel that Mary had not been unfaithful to him, he immediately married her, so that he took the blame for her pregnancy himself.

2. This also explains why the 'exception' is not in Mark or Luke. Both were written primarily for Gentile readers. Neither Greek nor Roman culture required virginity before marriage nor were there any penalties for its loss. These Gospel authors may have recollected Jesus' exception but saw no need to record it.

3. This also explains the astonished reaction to Jesus' teaching on the part of his disciples (Matthew 19:10 – 'If this is the situation between a husband and wife, it is better not to marry').

Had Jesus simply agreed with the conservative rabbi Shammai (adultery only) as against the liberal rabbi Hillel (for any cause), that might have been expected and accepted by his disciples. But if they understood him to mean only something that happened before the marriage could dissolve the bond and nothing after, the tone and content of their comment is entirely understandable. If marriage is impossible to get out of, better not get into it!

We have already noted that Matthew's version of the private conversation with the disciples following the public controversy with the Pharisees is totally different from Mark's. They are complementary rather than contradictory, recording consecutive sections of the discussion. In Matthew Jesus moves on to an extended treatment of celibacy, which is at such a tangent to the main theme of divorce that some scholars think it has come from another context. That is because they have misunderstood the next thing Jesus said.

His unexpected reply to the shocked and shocking conclusion of the disciples was, literally: 'not all are accepting that word' (Greek: *logos*). Whose 'word' (saying/talk/reasoning) is he referring to, his or theirs? Many say it refers back to his (in verses 8-9), which is encouraged by the New International Version's translation of 'logos' as 'teaching'. But this destroys the flow in Jesus' remarks. Referring to the disciple's reaction makes better sense of what follows.

The disciples assume celibacy is an easy option, a simple choice of the internal will. In saying singleness is given, Jesus is emphasising the need for an external factor to sustain what is a less natural and more difficult way of life than marriage. Some have been given a natural singleness from birth. Others have been made to be single by others (including no opportunity of marriage as well as amputation). Yet others have been given the grace to renounce (a costly action) marriage for the sake of the prior cause of the kingdom of heaven, as Jesus himself was. The statement is introduced and concluded with the same verb: 'The one *able* to accept, let him accept (celibacy).' Jesus is implying that marriage is the normal option for most people, even though the disciples see it as a life sentence.

4. It reduces the tension felt between Matthew on the one hand and Mark/Luke on the other. If 'fornication' refers to premarital promiscuity, then the Synoptic Gospels are in agreement. *Nothing* arising after marriage can justify divorce and therefore *all* remarriages after divorce are adulterous. Jesus' standards are absolute, not relative.

To many this will seem 'harsh', 'cruel' and 'lacking compassion', all of which have been said about preachers upholding it. But Matthew himself records Jesus as demanding a higher 'righteousness' than that of the strictest Jews and as applying even the ten commandments in a severer way. His compassion never led him to lower his standards to the level of people but to do everything he could, even dying, to lift them to his standards. His followers must do the same.

The reader may not be totally convinced by the case presented for the third interpretation of the 'except' clause, but at least a seed of doubt about the traditional position may have been sown. If so, we may ask: 'to whom should we give the benefit of the doubt, our Lord or us, who are so eager to justify ourselves?'

Author's note: Back in the 1960s I was chosen to sit on the Evangelical Alliance Commission on Divorce, to consider the proposed change in English law from 'proven cause' to 'irretrievable breakdown'. When I made known my view on 'fornication' in the 'except' clause, I was asked to prepare a paper on the subject for the next meeting, which I duly delivered. However, the chairman, John Stott, took the 'adultery' position and the majority agreed with him; this was eventually included in the Report. As the youngest present, I did not have the courage to press for a Minority Statement to be included, a failure I regret to this day. We were unanimous in our expectation that the new legislation would result in a considerable increase in the number of divorces, as it has proved to be.

Note

For readers who want a more detailed investigation into the meaning and usage of 'fornication' in classical Greek, the New Testament and early Church history, there is an excellent piece of research in the book by Daniel R Jennings: *Except for Fornication*, published by Sean Multimedia, at www.seanmultimedia.com. The sub-title is: *Why Evangelicals Must Reevaluate their Interpretation of Matthew's Divorce Exception Clause*. He makes a convincing case for limiting fornication to single sinners.

3. HIS EXAMPLE (John)

All Bible students are aware of the contrast between the 'Synoptic' Gospels (Matthew, Mark and Luke) and John, often called 'the Fourth Gospel' (it comes fourth in the Bible and was the fourth to be written, long after the others). The difference can be described in a number of ways. They all contain parables of the kingdom which are missing from his. His contains the great 'I am' sayings which are missing from theirs. They are records of what Jesus *did* and *said*. He is more concerned with what Jesus *was*.

John is the only Gospel author to declare his purpose (20:30). This is usually misunderstood by a failure to notice the tense of the verbs in the verse, which is the 'present continuous' Greek form, which means to continue doing something. He was not writing to persuade unbelievers to begin to believe, but to help believers to go on believing, that he *was* the Son of God; and going on believing they would go on having life (the same tenses can be found in 3:16). He was writing in Ephesus to counteract a heresy taught by Cerinthus, claiming that Jesus was neither fully human nor fully divine but somewhere in between! To support his divinity, John used seven witnesses (from John the Baptist to Thomas), seven miracles (all more spectacularly 'godlike' than those in the Synoptics) and seven statements about himself (from 'bread of heaven' to 'way', 'truth' and 'life').

But the difference that concerns us here is the change from crowds to individuals. Jesus dealt with both and some of his most memorable messages were given to just one person. Two examples spring to mind: the woman at the well and the woman caught in adultery.

John 4:4-42 (read)

Samaritans were the result of mixed marriages, between Jews who escaped the deportations of Israel to Assyria and Judah to Babylon, and remaining Canaanites still in the land. Jews returning from exile despised and even hated them, so much so that Galilean pilgrims to Jerusalem would take the much longer route via the east bank of the Jordan rather than go through Samaria, crossing back again at Jericho. All of which makes the parable of the good Samaritan very poignant and challenging.

Jesus 'had' to take the short cut (we are not told why), which brought him face to face with a bad Samaritan. She had come to draw water from a well at the hottest time of day, possibly to avoid meeting others. Surprised to be asked for a drink of water by Jesus (because, as John explains: 'Jews do not use utensils Samaritans have used'), he then told her about his own ability and willingness to give her a drink of superior liquid, 'living water'. He was referring to the Holy Spirit (7:39), but she didn't want to know that, so made a flippant and evasive joke about her daily trip to the well.

It was time to get serious and personal. On being told to bring her husband to meet Jesus, she said she didn't have one. In an unexpected 'word of knowledge', she was told she had already been through five of them and was now cohabiting with another man. This accurate exposure convinced her she might be talking to the expected Messiah and rushed off to share her discovery, eventually leading to a mini revival among the Samaritans, who showed themselves 'ripe for harvesting'.

We are not told how she 'lost' five husbands. It is highly unlikely that she was bereaved five times. At least some, if not all, were by divorce. Certainly she was sinning against the Mosaic law (which Samaritans adhered to as well as Jews; they do to this day). Cohabiting was fornication. Why was she not married to man number six? Perhaps she was not yet divorced from number five. Whatever, her lifestyle had been, and still was, illegitimate.

What we dearly want to know is *whether* Jesus counselled her about her relationships and if so, *what* he told her to do to put the situation right in the sight of the righteous God. Frustratingly, we are not told! There are so many possibilities. He could have told her to go back to husband 5, or 4, 3, 2 or 1. Or to marry No. 6 or to remain celibate from then on. Or to find a new man who believed in Jesus. Or even that because she was such a successful evangelist his rules on divorce and remarriage were waived in her case (a possibility which may seem ludicrous but has been presented to the author).

That we are not told may be due to the fact that John's purpose is to highlight the person, who and what he is, rather than to pass on his instructions for life to his apostles. The Samaritan situation is an illustration (read again verses 25-29 and 42).

There may be a further reason why John included so little information about the woman's personal recovery. The Holy Spirit did not want us to have anything like a legal precedent we could apply to similar situations. Human nature prefers to follow a compendium of solutions rather than wrestle with the application of wisdom. Christ is our wisdom (1 Corinthians 1:30).

However, let us turn to another narrative which does include Jesus' counsel to another immoral woman.

John 8:2-11 (read)

The first thing to be said about this moving incident is that it is not as well attested as the rest of John's Gospel. The earliest Greek manuscripts do not include it, as some translations note in a footnote. But it rings so true to Jesus' characteristic attitude and actions that most preachers do not hesitate to quote it as authentic. Yet few of them appreciate what Jesus was doing for the woman because they lack Jewish insights.

Most realise that in dragging the guilty woman to Jesus they were after him rather than her. It was a 'trap', facing him with an apparently impossible choice. The law of Moses certainly demanded the death penalty by stoning, for adultery. If Jesus opposed it in her case (did they suspect he would?), he could be accused by the Jews of dishonouring that law. If he approved it, he would be accused by the Romans of disobeying their law, which demanded exclusive rights to capital punishment. Either way, Jesus would be in real trouble.

The focus is not on the woman but on Jesus himself and his wisdom, which enabled him to escape from the trap without incriminating himself. He proved himself a better lawyer than his opponents (a lesson which was certainly consistent with the aim of the whole Gospel). He could have used the legislation that required the death of *both* the man and the woman caught in adultery (Deuteronomy 22:22), and the woman had been apprehended in the very act. It was a bad case of male chauvinism.

Instead he appealed to a legal custom in Jewish culture that no-one could be a witness for the prosecution who had been guilty of the same crime as the accused. Too many have thought 'without sin' meant of any kind. Only the morally perfect can ever administer punishment. That would spell the end of all application of justice! No policeman, no parent could ever fulfil their responsibility. Yet Jesus' statement is usually quoted in such a way that all retribution should be abandoned. No, he was saying to the woman's accusers: 'if you have never engaged in illicit sex, you are fit to judge and punish her! Significantly, the older ones admitted their guilt readily, while the younger tried to brazen it out. Yet even they eventually left. Incidentally, this principle that no-one who is guilty of the *same* misdemeanour has the right to judge another is written into the human conscience.

Meanwhile Jesus was stooping and writing with his finger in the dust by his feet. We are not told why he did this or what he wrote. Was it simply to remove his penetrating gaze from the dishevelled woman and her accusers, giving them time to consider their position? Or did it remind them that God had written the seventh commandment with his finger on the stone for Moses (Exodus 31:18)? Or was he suggesting that he himself had a hand, or at least a finger, in writing it? The reason for the inclusion of this detail is simply that he did it, whatever he intended by it. Such incidental particulars argue for the accuracy and authenticity of the record.

Jesus had avoided falling into the trap set for him. He had also rescued the woman from her dangerous predicament. To her he first addressed a double question, drawing attention to the absence of those who seized her, to which she gave the obvious answer. Then he gave her his own verdict and instruction.

Too much can be read into: 'Neither do I condemn you.' He was not saying she was forgiven, much less that she was now saved, though preachers love to see it this way. He was stating a simple fact, based on the Jewish law that such a serious case demanded the first-hand testimonies of 'two or three witnesses'. But they had all gone and Jesus was not one, even though he must have known she was guilty. So his words are simply equivalent to 'case dismissed'. There was simply nothing to answer.

This declaration of virtual innocence was followed by a sharp, clear and direct command to: 'Go and sin no more.' It is a call to real repentance, not faith. In simple terms: 'don't do it again'. There is also a subtle suggestion in the use of the Greek present continuous tense for the verb 'sin'. This had not been a momentary or occasional lapse but a regular habit with many or an ongoing relationship with one. Either way, at least one of them had been married, to qualify for the charge of adultery. The NIV has got it right with its translation: 'Leave your *life* of sin.'

It is an unequivocal command. It is a warning to abandon sinful relationships, lest worse befall. One can only speculate what Jesus would have said had she been brought back to him a few months later, having disobeyed his counsel, having resumed wrong relationships.

As we saw in the other Gospels, Jesus clearly taught that most if not all remarriages after divorce were committing (continuous) adultery! Would his directions for them be any different from what he said to this woman? Readers are left to draw their own conclusions.

6

WHAT PAUL SAID

It is fashionable in some quarters to drive a wedge between Jesus and Paul, to the detriment of the latter's influence on our beliefs and behaviour. He is even accused of complicating the 'simple' gospel taught by Jesus, making it more theological than practical, more doctrinal than dynamic. He has thus distorted 'Christianity', which needs to be rescued from his grip and restored to its original purity.

This questions his authority as well as his integrity. It suggests that his views carry less weight than those of Jesus (is this why some worshippers sit for the reading of the Epistles but stand for the Gospels?) Scholars have been quick to point out that Paul himself distinguishes between Jesus' teaching ('not I, but the Lord') and his own ('not the Lord, but I'), in a passage we shall consider in detail (1 Corinthians 7:10 and 12).

Yet Paul constantly defended his apostolic authority, derived from his direct call and commission by the risen, ascended Jesus. He also claimed to be inspired by the Holy Spirit (1 Corinthians 7:40). So he was not setting his counsel at the lower level of his 'opinion' only, but differentiating between what Jesus actually said on the subject, which he was quoting, and fresh revelation he had himself received, both of which are recognised as scripture, inspired and authoritative (cf. 2 Peter 3:16), carrying obligatory trust and obedience.

So Paul's words about our subject are here treated with equal seriousness to those of Jesus in the previous chapter. He will add new insights, but sourced in the same Spirit of truth. So they will always be complementary, never contradictory. Any inconsistency of interpretation or application is immediately suspect.

On divorce and remarriage, many claim Paul is more relaxed, more flexible, more 'liberal', more pastorally sensitive than Jesus! They say he has added another huge exception (desertion) to the sole one of Jesus (fornication). Some even say that he has removed *all* restrictions by saying that those 'released' from a marriage are not sinning if they remarry. And if anyone is already divorced and remarried when they come to faith, they should 'remain as they are'. All this is based on one chapter (1 Corinthians 7), which at first sight seems quite inconsistent with the 'Lord' Jesus' stern stand. It behoves us to tread very carefully through Paul's letters, making sure we really understand him. Three passages in particular need our attention:

Romans 7:1-6 (read)

These verses contain the unequivocal statement that 'a married woman is bound to her husband as long as he is alive'. The verb is worth noting (in Greek: *dedetai*). It is in the *perfect* tense, which means 'a past event with continuing effect', and is best translated: 'has been bound', a reference back to the wedding. There are no exceptions mentioned. Marriage is lifelong, which was also Jesus' position (Mark 10:6-9).

Surely that settles the matter. Marriage is indissoluble, except by the death of one partner. Yet some argue that this is not a necessary conclusion from this text, for the following reasons:

Paul has made a positive statement but has not followed up with the negative corollary that nothing or no-one else than death can dissolve a marriage. So he is not excluding other possibilities. But this is what we call 'an argument from silence', that is based on what has *not* been said, which is notoriously unreliable.

More impressive is the point that Paul is not here dealing directly with marriage or divorce but simply using it as an illustration, an analogy, for the wider truth that death liberates from legal restrictions, so Christ's death set him free and in him we are also set free from 'the law'. But we must point out that Paul's comparison is based on fact, not fiction. He is quoting 'the law' on marriage, which death dissolves, as the principle applying to all laws.

This raises the question of which 'law' he is quoting. He is referring to a 'law' with which his readers are familiar. Yet neither Greek nor Roman laws tied a couple for the rest of their lives. Divorce and remarriage were common in Gentile society. Nor can this be a reference to the Mosaic legislation, the Torah, which condoned and regulated divorce. Paul must be talking about God's original 'law' for marriage, which his Roman readers must have been informed about during their discipleship.

It seems appropriate to include this passage in our study. Though Paul's reference to marriage is incidental to his main argument, it could be important for that very reason, indicating that it may be taken for granted that marriage is for life.

1 Corinthians 7:1-40 (read)

Most of Paul's treatment of our topic is found here, so we must examine it with care, hoping to ascertain the understanding of both writer and readers of the original letter, which is not always easy.

We must begin with the wider culture and philosophy of Greece. 'Hellenistic dualism', as it is called, separated the spiritual aspect of life from the physical, elevating the former and downgrading the latter. The body was a handicap, even a prison, to the soul. Death released an immortal soul from the mortal body (almost the opposite of Christian thinking; 1 Corinthians 15:54).

This led to two opposing attitudes towards sexual behaviour: either promiscuity because the body did not affect the soul or asceticism because it did. Both extremes surfaced in Corinth. Being a seaport, prostitution was rife. Perhaps in reaction, there were some who advocated celibacy, even sexless marriage.

Believers were exposed to both pressures, enticing them back to former lifestyles even after repenting from them. Paul dealt with both in his letter. After dealing firmly with a case of incest, he moved on to the general use of prostitutes. Such indulgence, along with other sinful habits, could jeopardise their future inheritance of the coming kingdom of God. (In passing, note that fornicaters [*pornoi*] and adulterers [*moixoi*] are listed separately as quite distinct categories). That is because physical and spiritual are integrated by a God who is our Creator and our Redeemer. A Christian can actually link Christ with a prostitute (6:15)!

It is hardly surprising that some of the Corinthian believers reacted into a hyper-prudish attitude, welcoming teaching that 'it is good not to touch a woman' (the literal translation of 7:1). Many have taken this as a statement of Paul advocating celibacy, which he certainly does elsewhere in this chapter (NIV translates 'not to touch' as 'not to marry'). But the immediate context suggests otherwise. He is responding to a letter from Corinth and dealing with a point they have raised and he goes straight on to emphasise the duty and necessity of sexual intercourse within marriage. It therefore makes much more sense to take verse 1 as an example of extreme ascetic teaching invading the Corinthian fellowship, about which his correspondents are seeking his opinion. 'Touch' is therefore a euphemism for sex, and they have been told that all gratification, even within marriage, inhibits spiritual development (as, in our day, Mahatma Ghandi came to believe and practise). 'It is *good* not to...' may be taken to mean 'beneficial' rather than morally right, as for celibacy in verse 8. Perhaps 'better' would be preferable to 'good' in this instance.

Perhaps they expected Paul to agree with this advice, knowing he was single and that he advocated celibacy. It must have come as a surprise that he encouraged the physical side of marriage. The idea that each partner's body *belonged* to the other, especially the husband's to the wife, was revolutionary. Paul put strict restrictions on any sexual abstinence within marriage. It must be mutually acceptable, temporary and for a spiritual purpose. A unilateral denial of sexual satisfaction gave the devil an opportunity to destroy the marriage (one of the very few times Paul mentions Satan). Sex is both an essential element and a mutual obligation. But its exercise must be kept exclusively within a marriage. Note 'his own' and 'her own'. Denying satisfaction only puts a strain on self-control and encourages looking elsewhere.

Paul adds that his view is 'a concession, not a command', which seems to refer back to his advice on temporary, mutually agreed abstinence, which is not a compulsory requirement in a Christian marriage, but entirely voluntary. In his own case, he abstains from marriage and therefore sex altogether and wishes everybody else would, but he recognises that both states require a 'gift from God' to be successful.

Having dealt with the Corinthian query, Paul raises other matters, involving marriage and divorce, though nothing about remarriage after divorce, as we shall see. Having addressed them all so far, Paul now turns his attention to specific groups.

First, he has a word for those who are not married, either because they never have been or because their spouse has died. He recommends them to stay as they are ('as I am', for the second time). This is the 'good' course, again meaning better rather than right. But Paul is a realist, recognising the strength of sexual desire and the degree of self-control needed to restrain or sublimate it. That lies behind his notorious advice: 'better to marry than burn'.

This is neither the sole nor the prime reason for seeking a partner but it is certainly a real factor. Marriage is the God-given and God-intended outlet for this basic urge. Failure to control it can wreak havoc in human society and the very name 'Corinth' had become a byword for the moral chaos that ensues. Paul is not presenting marriage as the 'lesser of two evils', as some charge him with, but as the divine solution to the problem.

Second, he speaks to the married. This is a critical section for our subject. There are noticeable changes from the previous paragraph. His tone is admonitory rather than advisory, command rather than counsel, from you *may* to you *must*. And his authority switches from himself and his own wisdom to the Lord Jesus and his teaching, which he is now quoting.

He applies this to both wives and husbands separately and in that order. Quite simply, divorce is out. It is not an option. Nor are there any exceptions. Christian couples 'must not' separate. It is out of the question. Nothing could be clearer.

However, in between the absolute prohibitions to the partners is another statement which seems to be an exception! It is addressed to the woman rather than the man and begins: 'but if she *does* separate' (which is a synonym for divorce). This is an unfortunate and misleading translation, ignoring the tense of the verb, which is 'perfect' (used of a past event with ongoing effect). The phrase should be rendered: 'but if she has *already* separated'. This probably refers to before her conversion, only possibly before hearing Christian teaching on the subject.

Whatever, only two options are open to her, remaining single *or* reconciliation with her former husband. If the latter is not possible (if he has remarried, for example), then it must be celibacy. Remarriage is forbidden. The Gospels don't actually record Jesus mentioning this circumstance but it is a logical inference from his general stance, so Paul can include it here.

He now turns to 'the rest'. This phrase can hardly mean the rest of his readers. Having written to the unmarried and the married he has covered them all! So this probably refers to the rest of the Corinthian queries in their letter to him. Certainly he now deals with more specific cases within the two main married and unmarried categories, so:

Third, he tackles 'mixed' marriages, between believers and unbelievers. Of course these should not have happened at all. Christians, like Jews, should not marry outside God's people (Exodus 34:16; Malachi 2:11-12; 1 Corinthians 7:39; 2 Corinthians 6:14), but some still do. In some cases the unbeliever has made a profession of faith before the marriage which is revealed to be unreal after. Far more likely, Paul is thinking about one partner's conversion after the marriage, finding themselves in an 'unequal yoke' that was not intended.

Paul is concerned that the believer does not develop a guilty conscience about this and think about separating from their unbelieving partner. If they are willing to stay, the believer must also stay in what God regards as 'holy matrimony'. It is a sacred, not a secular, relationship in his sight, to be kept intact by the believer, if possible. The unbeliever is 'sanctified' by the believer. This does not mean they are saved or that they are living holy lives. But it does mean they are no longer in the 'unholy' category from which a believer must be separated to avoid being contaminated. Logically, if the believer thinks they are being polluted by the partner and must separate from them, then any children must also be defiled and must also be abandoned. Summing it all up, the believer is *never* justified for initiating divorce proceedings for 'spiritual', or any other, reasons.

But what if the unbeliever wants out? He or she never wanted such an intimate relationship with a Christian and may well be horrified to find themselves in bed with one! They could feel embarrassed, ashamed, even offended by the association. They could pass beyond this to hostility and hatred. It could certainly lead to disagreements and discord in the home, behind or in front of the children.

Paul's unexpected counsel is to let them go, to give them a divorce if they want one. He has just told Christians not to break up a marriage because it is 'holy' and is now advising them to do so! But the circumstances have changed. In the former case the unbeliever was willing to stay; now they are unwilling. The will is the fundamental factor in a marriage (hence the crucial words in modern ceremonies: 'I will'). Forced marriages without consent are not God's will.

Wisdom is flexible and adapts to situations (though never losing sight of fixed moral principles). Paul's apparently contradictory advice is actually consistent. Where the unbelieving partner is willing to stay, he fears that the believer will think it is their duty to go. Where the unbeliever wants to go, he fears that the believer will think it is their duty to stay. That is, they must do everything within their power to keep the marriage together as holy to the Lord, by opposing the unbeliever's will with their own. One example would be by refusing to co-operate in a divorce. Paul gives three reasons why any such reluctance is inappropriate.

First, marriage is not slavery. 'A believing man or woman is *not bound* in such circumstances' (verse 15). This statement has been so misinterpreted and misapplied that we must first realise what Paul is *not* saying. It was in the fifteenth century after Christ that the Christian humanist Erasmus, seeking a more 'humane' approach to divorcees, found here an additional 'exception' to Jesus' strict prohibition of divorce and remarriage, namely desertion. This was accepted by the Protestant Reformers of his day, led by Luther. From them it has entered evangelical tradition and is known as 'the Erasmian exception'. Scripturally speaking it could only apply to the case of an unbeliever leaving a believer, but many have made it more general, even extending it to an abandoning believer. However, this rests on the assumption that Paul is referring to the believer's *future* state and is 'not bound' to remain single but is free to remarry, finding another more congenial.

Unfortunately, English translations usually ignore both the tense of the verb and the verb itself. The tense is past, not present or future (actually, the 'perfect', again referring to a past event with continuing effect) and should be translated: 'were not bound'. Paul is referring to the first wedding, not discussing the possibility of a second, as contemporary scholars agree (see, for example, Gordon Fee's definitive volume in the New International

Commentary series published by Eerdmans).

Furthermore, the verb is quite different to the verb (*deo*) and noun (*desmos*) always used for marriage. It is *douleuo*, taken from the world of slavery (slave is *doulos*), never used of marriage. So it should be translated: 'you were not *enslaved*', i.e. in your marriage. A Christian slave has a duty to remain in that bond, which is why Paul sent Onesimus back to Philemon. But marriage is quite different. It is a bond but not bondage, which is the nearest we can get to the distinction in English.

This makes much better sense in its context. It is the first of three reasons why the believer should not try to make the unbeliever stay in the marriage.

Second, God has called us to live in peace. He is the 'God of peace' and wants us to be the same. Harmony is primarily due to wills in agreement and nothing destroys it more quickly than one person imposing their will on someone else, against their will (or their 'won't'!). Again, this reinforces Paul's wise advice to let the unbeliever go.

Third, holding on to an unwilling partner may not lead to their salvation. Paul is anticipating an objection to his advice: 'But I'm his only link with Christianity; if I let him go, he may be lost for eternity.' Paul therefore asks: 'How do you know you will be the means of his salvation?' Some think he expects a positive answer, which would argue for holding on to the marriage. But the context requires a negative response (I don't know), therefore another reason for letting them go. In fact, this is more likely to keep them sympathetic towards Christians than trying to force them to stay.

In all of this, Paul acknowledges that he cannot quote

the teaching of Jesus, who never spoke about mixed marriages, so far as we know. Hence the introductory phrase: 'I, not the Lord'. But this does not mean it can be dismissed as 'only his opinion'. He will conclude his section on marriage issues with: 'and I think that I too have the Spirit of God', who is the divine source of 'words of wisdom', to say nothing of his apostolic authority. His 'judgements' are, by the Lord's mercy, trustworthy (verse 25).

At this point, Paul moves on to a more general issue, prompted by the discussion of mixed marriages and the believer's responsibility to stay in what may not be an easy or congenial situation, unless the unbeliever wants to leave. He turns to the wider problem of 'itchy feet' in believers, especially new converts. Having found a new faith and a new life, it is quite common to want to exercise them in a new environment, more sympathetic or even more stimulating. This is particularly true of young converts, who imagine they could be better Christians in another environment (Bible College or even the mission field!), an illusion encouraged by some youth workers. The problem has been there from the beginning.

We have already noted a refrain running through this whole chapter: 'stay where you are'. In what is almost a parenthesis, Paul reinforces this counsel. God wants us to remain in the situation in which he called us until he tells us to move. Paul illustrates this from Jewish and Gentile culture, circumcision and slavery. By 'not become uncircumcised' he cannot mean transplanting a foreskin! It is a euphemism for abandoning Hebrew culture, based on the Torah.

This does not mean a permanent acceptance of one's 'station' in life for the rest of one's life. A slave may gain his freedom legitimately and should do so. And a free believer should never sell himself into slavery. Nor does it mean that a Christian must stay in employment that is immoral or illegal (for example, in a brothel or casino).

To sum up, the situation God called you *in*, is normally the situation God has called you *to*. Some have taken this to apply to a convert who has been divorced and remarried, implying that they stay with the latest partner. However, as we have already pointed out, Paul does not deal with the question of remarriage after divorce at all, though some say he does in the next paragraph, to which we now turn.

The next special group he addresses are those who are not married. For the third time in this chapter (verses 7, 8, 26) he urges them to remain single, as a 'good' (not right, but helpful) thing to be. For the first time he gives a reason for the choice: the 'present crisis', without specifying what this is, whether existential (a local, temporary one, like a famine) or eschatological (universal and final, this 'present evil age' of conflict between the kingdoms of God and Satan, ending in judgement). The latter is more probable. Paul was very aware of the crisis resulting from Jesus' first advent which will last until his second.

He now repeats his exhortation to 'remain' single in the form of two rhetorical questions and answers, the first of which is quite straightforward (those who are married should not seek to be 'released'). The second has proved very controversial (those who have been 'released', same word, should not seek to be married). Usually, the same word in the same context carries the same meaning. Since that is obviously 'divorced' in the first couplet, many assume the verb (Greek *luo* = to loose) means 'divorced' in the second.

There would be no problem had Paul not immediately added a qualification: 'but if you do marry, you have not sinned'. At first sight, it seems Paul is giving permission, if not approval, to remarriage after divorce. This would be a blatant contradiction of what he says both earlier (verse 8: 'she must remain unmarried or be reconciled to her husband') and later (verse 39: 'a woman is bound to her husband as long as he lives'). He would also be denying the validity of his Lord's teaching. He does admit that Jews never 'commanded' celibacy so Paul does not make it a requirement, only a recommendation (verse 25); but he would surely never go so far as to disagree with Jesus on such a fundamental issue.

So what is the solution to this dilemma? The only possibility is that Paul is using the verb 'released' in two different ways, not in its *effect* (what is the release *for*) but in its *cause* (what is the release *by*). In the first answer 'released' means 'divorced' and in the second it means 'bereaved'. What unites the two parties is that both are eligible in God's sight to be married.

Paul began this section by addressing 'virgins' who have never been married, then included those who have been married but are now free to marry again. His advice to both groups is the same. Positively, it would be better for them to remain single; negatively, it would not be wrong for them to marry (he repeats the latter for both).

He now enlarges on his reasons for recommending celibacy. He has already mentioned the 'present crisis' and the following verses confirm this as universal and permanent rather than local and temporary. A new age has dawned which will supercede the present one. A new world is on its way to replace this one, the days of which are numbered. Believers should be preparing for that one rather than getting immersed in this one. 'The time is short', both for the world outside us and individuals within it. And eternity is much longer.

All believers need this reminder. It is too easy to give so much time and attention to the here and now that the there and then is neglected by default. We get too involved in what is only temporary after all, including marriage. Paul sharpens his warning by employing the figure of speech we call hyperbole (exaggeration for sake of effect), as did the Lord Jesus (Matthew 5:29-30, clearly meaning drastic control of what we look at or handle rather than physical amputation). Paul exhorts the married to live as if they were single which, taken literally, would cancel out his counsel in verses 3-5. He seems to ban basic emotional reactions of sadness or happiness to anything that happens in this life! His exhortation is a little more 'realistic' by telling their readers they may buy things but must not regard them as property since all will be left behind. The final exhortation sums it all up. Use this world but don't become *engrossed* (Greek *kataxraomai* = to make total use of, to be consumed by) in it. We must not let our physical senses tie us down to a world that is not here for ever and this includes marriage, as the phrase: 'till death us do part' reminds us. To make our family or property the biggest thing in life is a fundamental mistake, leaving us ill-prepared for the future. Living for the present (existentialism) is a destructive way of life!

To this larger reason for advocating celibacy for those eligible to marry, Paul adds a lesser one that can be a real pressure on the married, namely distraction from the work of the kingdom by family responsibilities for spouse and children. A single person can concentrate on pleasing the Lord but the married must also consider pleasing their partner, which can create conflict. Life is more complicated when there are divided loyalties, as many married servants of God could testify (and this may explain the increased divorce rate among them).

Paul now addresses another special group, those who are engaged to be married. It is not *wrong* for this to be consummated, especially if the woman is getting on in years, diminishing her chance of finding someone else if the wedding is called off. But if the man has become convinced he ought to remain single and is in full control of his passion, then breaking the engagement is the *right* thing to do. Again, Paul reiterates his conviction that marriage is right, but celibacy is better (very rarely preached or practised in our sex-obsessed society today).

In summarising his comments on marriage (and singleness), Paul repeats the most fundamental premise, that only the death of a partner dissolves a marriage. Otherwise, the marriage bond (not bondage) remains intact in the sight of the Lord. But the surviving partner (more often than not the wife, then as now) is then completely free to marry again. The only restriction is that the new husband must be a fellow-believer, even if the first never was or became one. The desire for renewed companionship or sexual satisfaction must not overrule this.

But Paul must yet again slip in his opinion that she will be 'better' off to remain single, adding that he believes it has been divinely inspired.

Throughout, Paul has stood firmly with Jesus in his prohibition of divorce and remarriage. We have shown that those who find 'loopholes' for remarried divorcees (in verse 15 for some and verse 28 for all) are misinterpreting the text, especially the tense of the verbs which look back to the past rather than around in the present or forward to the future, the first marriage rather than a second.

1 Timothy 3:1-13 (read)

The only phrase in these lists of qualifications required in those who act in the church as elders or deacons (ideally, 'supervisors' or 'servants') is that they be 'husband(s) of one wife'.

This is not because there is a higher standard for 'officers' in the church than for ordinary members but because their position carries the responsibility of being a clear example of what all are called to be. They should not be appointed until they are.

But what does 'one wife' mean? The New International Version has inserted an additional word ('*but* one wife') which gives added emphasis but could be misleading. There are three possibilities, revealed by considering what the phrase is excluding.

First, the most obvious alternative is polygamy, having more than one wife at the same time. We have already noted God's intention of marriage being for one man and one woman (in Genesis 2:24). Since redemption is the restoration of creation to its original condition, it almost goes without saying that monogamy is the norm for Christians. Second, it has been understood to prohibit any more than one marriage in a lifetime. Christian ministers should have been married only once, even if their spouse has died. This seems excessively restrictive in the light of other scriptures which freely accept remarriage after bereavement (Romans 7:2; 1 Corinthians 7:39; 1 Timothy 5:14). However, the early church 'Fathers' seem to have taken it this way, though that doesn't mean they were right.

Third, it forbids divorce and remarriage. To have another wife while the first is still alive would amount to bigamy or consecutive polygamy in the Lord's eyes even though it was all done legally. It would certainly be a bad example to the flock.

Relating this to the rest of the New Testament, the third possible meaning would make most sense and is therefore favoured by this author.

In passing, it may seem frivolous to point out that women can hardly be 'husbands of one wife'. This suggests that the ministry was limited to the male gender, at least in the case of eldership. The reference to 'women' in verse 11 may allow for deaconesses (the word *diakonos* is applied to Phoebe in Romans 16:1). For a full discussion of the roles and responsibilities of men and women in the Church, see the author's book *Leadership is Male*, published by Terra Nova Publications. This concludes our study of 'What Paul Said'.

7

WHAT THE CHURCH HAS SAID

Back to short chapters! There are a number of reasons for this change of pace:

One is that the author is a Bible teacher, not a Church historian, so is not really qualified in this field. Another is that he is an evangelical Christian, not a liberal, Catholic or Orthodox. Therefore the authority of the Bible far outweighs that of the Church. Scripture is the final arbiter in all matters of Christian belief and behaviour, overriding tradition.

So this will be only a brief sketch of some of the changes in attitude towards marriage, divorce and remarriage in ecclesiastical circles over the centuries.

The reader may be surprised by the variety of opinion that emerges. This has led to the current differences, which enable couples to 'shop around' until they find a church that accepts and agrees with them! In turn, this makes nonsense of church discipline, encouraging its neglect.

How can churches using the same Bible come to such a diversity of principle and practice? There are two major causes:

The *most obvious* is a departure from scriptural

standards. An increasing number of church leaders regard them as 'culturally conditioned' by the situations in which they were given and they can be adapted, indeed must be adapted to fit contemporary society. They sincerely believe that a church clinging to past norms will lose its present credibility and future prospects. At worst, this outlook is based on the concept of a flexible God whose only constant is his love. At best, it is an attempt to make the gospel more relevant and acceptable to the modern world. Either way, it succeeds only in changing the gospel itself.

The *more subtle* is to impose a particular way of thinking on the scripture, which predetermines the results. This may be illustrated by just one Bible word: 'covenant', used of God's unique dealings with humans. How many covenants has he made? The answers range from one to seven! On these depend the direct relevance of different parts of the Bible to Christian believers.

Since the Protestant Reformation, for example, much 'Reformed' doctrine has assumed there is only *one* 'covenant of grace', as they call it, though that phrase is never found in scripture. It means that the Old and New Testament requirements are all binding on Christian believers, maybe changed in form but not significance (circumcision becomes baptism, still applied to babies; the sabbath becomes Sunday, etc.). Deuteronomy 24 still applies to remarriage after divorce.

At the opposite end of the spectrum, 'Dispensational' doctrine divides history into *seven* eras, in each of which God demands different ethical requirements. Even the Sermon on the Mount, with its teaching on divorce, is assigned to a future 'Kingdom' era called 'the Millennium', Deuteronomy is consigned to a past epoch of 'Law'. Neither is for the 'Church' era.

In between are many ordinary Bible readers misled by the titles given to the two sections of the Bible ('testament' is a synonym for 'covenant'). The 'Old' is of historical interest and the 'New' is of timeless relevance. They study one but live by the other.

This author believes there are *five* major covenants in the Bible, named after the five individuals with whom God first made them: the Noahic, the Abrahamic, the Mosaic, the Davidic and the Messianic. All five figure in both Testaments. Only one is called 'old' (the Mosaic) and only one is called 'new' (the Messianic). The latter has replaced the former but none of the others. The author has expanded this thesis to a whole chapter in his book *Defending Christian Zionism* (an attitude towards the Jewish people and their land which assumes that the Abrahamic covenant promises have not been changed, much less cancelled; see Galatians 3:17-18; Hebrews 6:13-18). So four of the five covenants involve Christians.

The number of covenants thought to be in scripture and directly related to Christians has a profound effect on its interpretation and application (together called 'hermeneutics'). It is time to turn to our survey of church history, which we *can* divide into eras, the early, imperial, medieval, Reformation and modern.

THE EARLY ERA

When the Church spread from its Jewish birthplace into the Greek-Roman world, it encountered a culture in which divorce and remarriage were commonplace. Hardly surprising, then, that the 'Church Fathers' (as the teachers in the first few centuries were called) said quite a lot relating to our theme, in fact even more than on the second coming of the Lord Jesus to earth!

There does seem to be a general consensus among them, which may be summarised as follows. They allowed divorce among Christians, strictly on the sole ground of persistent adultery, but, unlike the Jews, they did not approve of remarriage after such divorce. They even frowned on remarriage after bereavement, especially among elders.

Names behind this rather unusual position were Hermes, Justin Martyr, Clement, Origen, Basil, Ambrose and Jerome. There were one or two dissidents, like Ambrosiaster and Athenagoras. The latter taught that marriage was for eternity (not dissimilar to modern Mormon ideas) and therefore totally indissoluble.

Summing up, most divorces and all remarriages were regarded as sinful and discipline was exercised accordingly.

THE IMPERIAL ERA

The professed 'conversion' of the Roman emperor Constantine brought a radical change. Christianity became, for the first time, a religion 'established' by law. Church and State were drawn together in an uneasy alliance, which has remained to this day in many European countries. State laws began to reflect Christian standards, but the influence was not just one way. As the Church was allied to the world, worldliness entered the Church, even in the Church's leadership, which became more modelled on the empire than the New Testament (for example, many 'bishops' in each local church became one regional bishop over many churches, and finally one bishop (in Rome) was 'father' (papa, pope) of the whole church, with regalia and titles (e.g. 'Pontifex Maximus') taken from former 'Caesars'. Hermits in the desert and monks in monasteries were a protest against this trend and celibacy began to be associated with holiness.

This was accelerated with the conversion of 'saint' Augustine, from a promiscuous lifestyle, including a mistress and illegitimate son, to be bishop of Hippo in North Africa and the most influential theologian, for better or worse, the Church has ever had. Partly because of reaction to his early lifestyle but more because of his education in Greek philosophy, particularly Platonism, he injected an anti-physical and anti-sexual prejudice into the main stream of Christian thinking which is still around today. Even within marriage, sex was said to be 'concupiscence' (lust), leading to a negative attitude to marriage, to say nothing of divorce and remarriage.

THE MEDIEVAL ERA

'Priests' by now were compelled to be celibate and thus were models of true holiness, at least in this regard!

Ironically, marriage had been elevated to one of seven 'sacraments', dispensed by the clergy to the laity. This was based on a textual mistranslation by Jerome in the Latin Vulgate version. He had rendered 'mystery' in Ephesians 5:32 (Greek, *musterion*) into the latin *sacramentum*. Originally describing the oath of allegiance taken by a Roman soldier towards his emperor, it had come to mean a 'means of grace' controlled by the Church.

Like some other sacraments (baptism and extreme unction for the dying), it was regarded as unrepeatable. Therefore marriage was 'indissoluble' and divorce absolutely prohibited, under pain of excommunication (it still is in the Roman Catholic Church).

Human nature is adept at locating loopholes in the law, and in this case it was found in the notion of 'annulment', which meant discovering and declaring a marriage never to have been 'proper' from the beginning, usually because of the presence of compulsion or the lack of consummation. That this seems to have been more readily available for those who could make substantial contributions to the Church's funds is a further comment on human nature. It was the pope's refusal to grant annulment to King Henry VIII that would spark the English Reformation.

THE REFORMATION ERA

There had been attempts to reform the Roman Church in England (e.g. John Wycliffe) and in Bohemia (Jan Hus), but it was in Germany (with Martin Luther) that the religious face of northern Europe was radically changed. His 'protesting' began with the abuse of 'Indulgences', selling reduced time in 'purgatory' (another Roman innovation) to pay for the building of St Peter's in Rome. It soon included many other distortions and abuses, judged in the light of scripture alone (*sola scriptura*) as the final authority over the Church. For example, Luther saw nothing in scripture demanding celibacy of 'priests', so he married a nun and encouraged others to follow. However, the change of attitude to divorce and remarriage came from Holland.

The Reformation coincided with another movement, beginning in Italy and called 'the Renaissance'. It was a rediscovery of Greek and Roman 'classical' culture. With it came an appeal to reason (Enlightenment), coupled with an optimistic view of human nature and ability (Humanism), which would later be the greatest challenge biblical Christianity had ever faced (e.g. the debate around creation and evolution, which still rages).

Some tried to combine these great movements and are referred to as 'Christian humanists'. Notable among them was Erasmus of Amsterdam. He published an edition of the Greek New Testament, which later Luther would use while in hiding to produce the first German Bible. It showed up weaknesses in the Latin version, the only text known up till then. He shared Luther's anger over Rome but split with him over whether reform should be by pressure inside or protest outside.

One of Erasmus's significant contributions to Protestant thinking was to find an extra 'exception' to divorce and remarriage. Troubled about the 'inhuman' attitude of Rome to divorcees, he searched the scriptures to see if he could relieve their plight and came across Paul's advice to the believer married to a hostile unbeliever. He believed that 'not bound' referred to the future and set the believer free to remarry. This became known as 'the Erasmian exception' and was adopted by most, but not all, of the Protestant Reformers. Though it was only at first applied to the departure of an unbeliever, it eventually became 'desertion' by any partner, even a believer.

This 'double exception' view persisted throughout the 'Puritan' epoch and was incorporated in their well-known 'Westminster Confession'. It is held by many Evangelicals today (see the writings of John R.W. Stott). At the same time, there is now a much wider diversity of opinion.

THE MODERN ERA

We are looking at the twentieth century and primarily at England, best known to the author. Here the feature of the ecclesiastical scene we will consider is the difference between the Church of England and the other (non Roman Catholic) denominations, i.e. the 'established' and the 'free' churches. This pattern is mirrored in other European regions, particularly in Lutheran Scandinavia in the north and some Catholic countries in the south.

1. ESTABLISHED

Born out of the king's break with the pope over his divorce and remarriage(s), it was perhaps inevitable that the Church of England would be beset with problems of sexual morality. Faulty foundations can eventually bring the whole structure down (as some would say is happening right now in the controversies over female and homosexual bishops).

Henry VIII, something of an amateur theologian, had written a book against Luther in his early years, for which the pope awarded him the title of 'Defender of the Faith', still borne by English sovereigns, even inscribed on English coins. After his defiant break with Rome and subsequent 'dissolution' (confiscation and destruction) of Roman monasteries in his realm, Henry became more sympathetic to the continental Protestants. During the next few reigns the Church staggered between Rome and Canterbury, under the preferences of successive monarchs, with bloody persecution on both sides. The 'Settlement' under Elizabeth I led to a unique blend (some would say a typical English muddle or at best an uneasy truce) of Catholic and Protestant spirituality. This has led to an 'umbrella' structure, boasting of being an inclusive 'family' of those who appeal to scripture (the 'low' wing), reason (the 'broad' wing) or tradition (the 'high' wing) as their prime authority. The 'high' came into prominence in the nineteenth century. Leadership was in the hands of the 'broad' in the twentieth century, but during the second half the 'low' became a significant influence at the grass-roots level. The spectrum becomes a kind of horseshoe shape when it comes to doctrinal and ethical standards, the 'high' and 'low' nearer to each other than either is to the 'broad'.

Inevitably, such inclusivism leads to controversy. There have been many Commissions on marriage, divorce and remarriage as the state laws have been relaxed, putting pressure on a church whose head is the reigning Sovereign, whose bishops are appointed by the Prime Minister (with advice) and whose ritual has to be approved by Parliament. What with political pressures from without and theological differences within, it is hardly surprising that there has been so much discussion and so little conviction relating to our topic.

In theory, 'Canon law' allows divorcees to be remarried in a parish church, though very few vicars actually do this, many pleading the bishop's approval or disapproval. Most refuse to conduct the ceremony, but offer a service of 'Prayer and Dedication after a Civil Marriage' (often colloquially referred to as a service of 'blessing') to be used after a wedding in a register office (or other licensed premises). This appears to many non-Anglicans as compromise, even hypocrisy. If God can bless the marriage, why can he not bless the ceremony? If he cannot bless the ceremony, how can he bless the marriage? The fact is, it is only the 'blessing of the church', keeping everyone happy and the consciences of couples and clergy clear.

2. FREE

Free of political restraint and in some cases free also of centralised control, the 'Free' churches have on the whole been more ready to change and 'adapt' to social developments. They also seem to have been free to accept the Enlightenment's fruit in German theology, the 'Higher Criticism' of scripture which questioned its supernatural source and content. (The 'Lower Criticism' was limited to the search for the most accurate original text by comparing the surviving manuscript copies.) So 'liberalism' invaded many Free Church pulpits.

One result was an increasing willingness to remarry divorcees, at first only those who were considered to be the 'innocent' party, but later the 'guilty' also. It is claimed that to do otherwise would be to make divorce the unforgivable sin and be contrary to divine compassion and forgiveness.

An increasing number of churches hold 'divorce recovery' courses seeking to help people get over what is a trauma comparable to bereavement; but the question of remarriage receives variable or ambiguous answers.

In the USA, where all churches are 'Free', divorce and remarriage are as common inside as outside the churches, even among the evangelicals claiming to believe and follow the Bible, pastors and members alike.

In Africa, Anglicans, who are both autonomous and indigenous, tend to be more conservative, and impatient with equivocation elsewhere in Anglicanism.

All this underlines the diversity of belief and practice within the body of Christ. Historians must be tearing their hair out over this chapter's potted and simplified overview of two thousand years, but it has been enough to demonstrate that reliance on the Church as one's infallible guide is a misguided and misleading exercise, especially when it seems to be following the spirit of the age rather than the Holy Spirit and the scriptures he inspired.

It is against this background that we have to formulate what we ought to be saying to our generation.

8

WHAT WE SHOULD SAY

This chapter is primarily written for preachers, teachers, counsellors, parents, indeed anyone who has the responsibility of passing on Christian ethical standards. Ignorance must be laid at their door.

Before looking at *what* needs to be communicated, there is the question of *when* to be considered. Far too often the issue is not raised until it crops up in a personal and highly emotional situation, when many feel it is too difficult or even too late to intervene.

It is therefore vital that it should be a regular part of any teaching curriculum, particularly in pulpits or on platforms of churches. The least offensive way of doing this is by systematic exposition of the Synoptic Gospels, when the subject comes up both inevitably and naturally. The only temptation here is that of referring to other Gospels at the same time (for example, while exegeting Mark's categorical stance to emphasise Matthew's exception).

Churches whose teaching ministry is more topical, often by having different speakers all the time, have the more difficult task of making sure it is included in the programme and finding someone willing to take it! There is the added problem of stimulating speculation about the reason for introducing it ('why now?' and 'who for?'). It is important to include the subject in any schedule for teens and twenties, the group most likely to be contemplating marriage. And especially in marriage preparation classes for individual couples or groups of the engaged (in a day of prenuptial agreements about the disposal of assets 'should it not work out'). Divorce and remarriage are now so widely accepted as normal that Christian youth can easily do the same unless forewarned.

So much for what we might call general instruction. There are two specific situations needing urgent intervention. Christian leaders can shrink from confrontation but rebuke is part of their calling (2 Timothy 4:2; Titus 2:15), even publicly (1 Timothy 5:20).

The first case is where Christian couples are considering divorce, either having fallen out of love with each other or in love with someone else. They need to be told about the difference between human and divine love (*eros* and *agape*), the seriousness of breaking covenant vows made before the Lord and, above all, that Christians who separate must remain single for the rest of their lives or be reconciled (1 Corinthians 7:11). However, it has been the author's experience that none of this counselling is likely to have much effect on those who have been taught that their salvation will never be in jeopardy (see my book: *Once Saved, Always Saved?* Hodder, 1996).

The second case is the most difficult of all to deal with, where couples have already gone ahead, divorced, and remarried. Many reasons (excuses?) have been put forward for not intervening in these circumstances, virtually claiming it is 'too late' to do or even say anything.

One is that it all happened before the couple became Christians. To some it therefore does not matter and belongs to the 'all is forgiven' past and is therefore irrelevant to church membership or leadership, which are for 'new creatures in Christ'. But we have already pointed out that conversion does not change our 'married' (or 'divorced') status; that God is involved with all marriages, whether they take place in a garden (Eden), a register office or a church, 'Christian' or otherwise; and that Jesus applied his strictures on divorce and remarriage to 'anyone'.

The time factor is often introduced as a mitigating circumstance. 'It all took place ten/twenty/thirty/forty years ago.' The assumption is that responsibility for past behaviour gradually fades as the years pass by. The final Judgement Day will come as a shock to many, when their whole lives will be under review. Memories and therefore consciences may become dim, though both can be revived by an encounter with mortality. But heavenly records cannot be erased by us, as will be evident when the books are opened (Revelation 20:12). Only God himself can 'blot out' anyone or anything from his records (Exodus 32:33; Revelation 3:5), which of course is the heart of the good news of the gospel (Jeremiah 31:34), for those who repent (Acts 3:19).

Perhaps the most poignant argument for condoning the situation is the consideration of innocent children. That is, where the remarriage has produced offspring, who could be badly affected by any challenge to the legitimacy of their parents' relationship. Interestingly, those who raise this difficulty rarely seem to be so concerned about children of previous marriages who were abandoned when divorce robbed them of a normal family life, but the concern to avoid a further such tragedy is understandable.

In spite of these objections the truth of the situation is better faced now than when all is revealed. Better to be embarrassed now than ashamed then.

Broadly speaking there are two approaches in counselling those already on the wrong side of the New Testament standard: precedent and principle. The first tends to be legalistic; the second is actually more loving.

PRECEDENT

English common law is largely based on precedent. Counsels for the prosecution and defence frequently appeal to previous trials when presenting their case, hoping for a similar verdict. Each judgement is added to the huge reservoir of records for future references. A lawyer's training involves memorising relevant examples.

This approach can be unwittingly transferred from the legal to the moral sphere. What have others done, especially if they have 'got away with it', suffered no ill consequences? 'If others have done it, so can I.'

Whenever this author has taken a seminar for clergy, ministers and pastors on this issue of divorce and remarriage, the questions have been dominated by tales of individual circumstances, sometimes quite lengthy, ending with: 'what would you do in this case?' I have long since realised they are hoping for a precedent which they can then quote, either from my wisdom, experience and knowledge, or that of others. What they want is a compendium of case histories which they can search for a parallel situation and how it was dealt with, which can then be applied to their own pastoral problems. It is so much easier to copy other people's practice than work out one's own!

This is what the Jews have done in such documents as the Midrash, Talmud, the Targums. Even in Jesus' day they had expanded the sabbath into dozens of detailed requirements and precise applications, which he classed as 'traditions of men'. If Christians followed suit, it would be both an extensive and expensive volume!

There are so many variable factors in any divorce. Who took the initiative, husband or wife? Were they both believers, neither, or one of each? What were the *real* reasons for the break-up (often more than one)? Who was the innocent party (not as simple an issue as it sounds)? Was it done in ignorance or disobedience? Were there any children involved? Was it a first, second or third marriage? What age were they? How long ago was it? Did others put pressure on them, to part or stay together? Similar queries may be made about the remarriage after divorce.

The complexities of each situation have led some counsellors to adopt a 'relativistic' attitude treating every case on its own merits (or demerits) and recommending the course which they feel is the best or 'least worst' in the circumstances. This flexibility has been given theological support by Fletcher's 'situational ethics', based on the premise that 'love is the only absolute' in Christian behaviour. This reduces problems to the simple issue of what is the most loving solution for all concerned. Of course, it depends on what is meant by 'love'! The danger of this approach is that it descends from the scriptural level to the sentimental.

The fact is that the New Testament does not contain a single precedent, not even in the case of the woman at the well in Samaria, which cries out for more information! We may deduce that God did not intend us to handle this issue in that way or he would have included some examples for us.

At the opposite extreme are those who believe that each situation is unique and different from others. Therefore there is no 'formula' for the counsel that needs to be given, just as there is no exact parallel that can be quoted. What is called for is *wisdom*. But there are two kinds of wisdom. Human wisdom comes from within, has been gained from long experience and usually suggests the *best* thing to do in a given situation. Divine wisdom comes from above (James 3:17) can be immediately inspired as 'a word of wisdom' (1 Corinthians 12:8) and focuses on the *right* thing to do in a given situation. It is therefore more directly related to moral principles, which must be applied in all circumstances. To be 'wise' in this way is to know how to apply them, never how to avoid them, for which the adjective 'clever' is more appropriate.

PRINCIPLE

There are four such 'principles' to be applied to those who have already divorced and remarried, namely: sin, repentance, forgiveness and discipline. The first three are essentially individual matters and the last corporate.

1. SIN

Vice is primarily something bad we do to ourselves; crime is primarily something bad we do to others; sin is primarily something bad we do to God. It is the choice to follow our own will rather than submit to his. It is to defy his moral standards and define our own. It is to 'fall short' of divine perfection. Accepting biblical definitions, few would argue with the biblical conclusion that 'there is no-one righteous, not even one' (Romans 3:10) and 'all have sinned' (Romans 3:23).

Realising this does not come naturally to us. We are adept at excusing (justifying) ourselves and blaming others. We need the help of both scripture and the Spirit quickening our conscience to be persuaded (convicted). This is one reason why God gave his laws to Israel: 'it is the straight edge of the law that shows us how crooked we are' (Romans 3:20, translated by J B Phillips in *Letters to Young Churches*).

Sin is breaking his commandments, of which the seventh in 'the Ten' forbids adultery. A simple syllogism follows:

Adultery is sin.

Jesus said remarriage after divorce is adultery.

Therefore such remarriages are sin.

But we live in an age of increasing reluctance to call sin 'sin'. The phrase 'living in sin' is no longer 'politically correct' and has become 'cohabiting with a partner'. Why is 'sin' so offensive?

For one thing, it reminds us of God. It is one of his words, not ours. We see human foibles as weaknesses or mistakes. He sees them as sins against himself and his creation.

For another, it reminds us of judgement. We will one day be accountable to him for our sins and because he is righteous he must punish sinners. This is no longer acceptable thinking. 'Retribution' has been replaced by 'rehabilitation', except in the most extreme inhumane crimes. 'Open prisons' (an oxymoron if ever there was one) begin to resemble holiday camps on full board. And as for an everlasting hell, how could the worst sinner deserve that?

So calling anything 'sin' is offensive, yet until behaviour is acknowledged as such, the gospel can neither be applied nor appreciated. It is only good news after it is bad news (Romans 1-3 comes before the other chapters). Only when this first principle has been understood can we move to the second:

2. REPENTANCE

In the name of 'Free Grace', some are now teaching that repentance is not essential for salvation and therefore not for forgiveness of sins. They must have problems with its prominence in the New Testament! Both John and his cousin Jesus called people to 'repent and believe'. Peter's first sermon on the day of Pentecost told the hearers to 'repent and be baptised'. Paul told the Athenians that God now commanded all people everywhere to repent.

But what does 'repent' actually mean? It certainly begins in *thought*, literally a change of mind ('re'- and 'pent', like 'pensive'). Seeing sins from God's point of view, hating sin as he does, is a radical shift in outlook.

Such conviction leads to confession, expressing sorrow and regret in *words*. But repentance is more than feeling or even saying sorry, and to be real and true will show in *deeds*, a change of lifestyle. John the Baptist demanded 'fruit worthy of repentance' and gave practical examples (Luke 3:7-14). Paul expected his converts to prove their repentance by their deeds (Acts 26:20). Would that all evangelists required the same today!

Just as faith without action is dead and cannot save (James 2:14-26), repentance is the same; both are something to *do*. Repentance involves a change of direction in life, a U-turn, away from sin and towards God. Its deeds will be both negative and positive.

The positive deeds of repentance involve putting right whatever can be put right. We call this 'restitution'. It ranges from apologies to those offended, through repayment of debts, to confession of crimes to the police. It brings peace to the conscience and even joy to the heart.

The negative deeds of repentance involve renunciation and reformation. This means abandoning anything from bad habits to wrong relationships. Those who despair of being able to do this will find that if they have genuinely come to share God's hatred of sin, he will give them his power to do so and 'grant them repentance' (Acts 11:18). The schoolboy's definition of repentance is as good as any: 'being sorry enough to stop'.

The New Testament contains stark warnings to any who knowingly persist in sinful behaviour after 'receiving knowledge of the truth' (Hebrews 10:20-31 is just one such passage). Very strong language accompanies these alarms. There is no available sacrifice for such deliberate disobedience (echoing the Levitical sacrifices which only applied to 'unintentional' sins; Leviticus 4:2, 13, 22, 27). The Son of God has been 'trampled underfoot'. The Spirit of grace has been insulted. The appropriate response to such awful consequences is to be afraid of falling 'into the hands of the living God' and into the 'raging fire' which consumes those who abuse his generosity.

This brings us to the very crux of the issue before us. What ought those already divorced and remarried to *do* about it? In the case of every other sin the simple answer is to get out of it. Take the eighth commandment: 'You shall not steal', which is right next to the one forbidding adultery. The New Testament endorses the prohibition: 'He who has been stealing *must* steal no longer' (Ephesians 4:28). Both were written before any welfare states, when poor families faced the choice: steal or starve, or worse, steal or watch your children starve. Many parents chose to steal, in spite of severe sanctions (it is not so long ago in England that the penalty for stealing a loaf of bread was execution by hanging). For a believer to pray the prayer Jesus taught his disciples ('Give us today our daily bread') required far more faith than it does now in the developed world and still does in many other regions. But for all believers, rich and poor, stealing is out. Earning is in, hopefully with enough for a lifestyle of giving to others, instead of taking from them (again Ephesians 4:28).

Yet there is an extraordinary reluctance in Christian leaders to apply the same logic to the 'adulterous' relationship of the divorced and remarried. Funnily enough, many would have no hesitation in dealing radically with a straight case of believers committing adultery, telling them to end it immediately and return to their partner. It seems as if a legal divorce followed by a legal marriage has completely changed the situation in the eyes of the Lord and a different category of adultery has now been entered, which need not be stopped.

At the very least, such couples need to be *absolutely* sure that the Lord has given them permission to continue 'living in sin'. The author has been faced with a number of claims that 'special revelations' have given exemption from the Lord's teaching. Some have even told me *before* the divorce that the Lord has told them to ditch their wife and marry someone who will be a better helper in ministry, only to receive my response: 'I don't know whether to call that rubbish or blasphemy.' I am prepared to believe that the God who made the rules is above them and can change them. But I am sceptical when his freedom to do so is so exactly in line with our own ideas and desires!

Every couple counselled has convinced themselves that they are an 'exception' in the eyes of the Lord, either by scriptural or individual revelation. So much so that the exceptions have become the rule and what Jesus thought would be a minority has become the majority. So we must turn to a third principle, one which is the most difficult to apply to the situation we are facing.

3. FORGIVENESS

This is the most amazing truth, that God himself is willing to forgive and forget our sins, to blot them out of his record, take them as far away from us as the east is from the west and bury them in the deepest sea. Scripture stretches the human vocabulary to its limit in describing the wonder of it.

However, it is easy to forget that it would be utterly immoral for a good God to do this unless our sins had already been paid for and his justice satisfied – by someone else on our behalf. And he sent his own Son to do just that, suffering the most extreme penalty man has ever devised for wrongdoing, the lingering, humiliating, 'excruciating' execution by crucifixion. Every act of divine forgiveness is written in the blood of Jesus. Pardon may be free for us but it was costly for him.

It cannot be said too strongly that neither divorce nor remarriage are unforgivable, though Christians have been accused of treating them as such. There is one 'unforgivable' sin, which is to call the work of God the work of the devil, to call good evil (and evil good?) until one can no longer discern the difference (see Matthew 12:22-32). So it is essential to assure couples who have divorced and remarried that full and final forgiveness is available to them. It can be as if it had never happened!

There seems to be little or no reluctance to apply this principle. Counsellors seem only too eager to offer such solace to those who are uneasy in conscience. It is done in the name of God's love and Jesus' compassion, both of which are part of the truth, but not the whole of it. When they are over-emphasised, at the cost of other truths, two mistakes are commonly made:

First, forgiveness becomes *isolated*. On the one hand, from sin, which we have already referred to. On the other hand, from holiness, which is also an essential element in the gospel offer. Forgiveness is not the end but the means to an end. By enabling us to be reconciled to God, it has opened the door to the possibility (not the inevitability) of becoming like him, holy as he is holy. To use theological terminology, justification is intended to lead to sanctification, which in turn will lead to glorification, the ultimate goal of our salvation. Rightly understood and appropriated, forgiveness is only the beginning of 'being saved' and leads on to so much more until the process is completed.

Second, forgiveness becomes *unconditional*. The adjective is nowhere to be found in scripture but in the last few decades has become firmly attached to God's love and, by implication, to his forgiveness. This is taken to mean that we can do nothing to deserve it (which is true) and that we need do nothing to receive it (which is not true). Forgiveness is not offered regardless of human response, or no-one would ever be 'sent' to hell (the Bible verb is 'thrown', as for discarded rubbish) and that awful fire becomes no more than a non-existent threat.

This seems a good point to introduce the fourth principle to be applied.

4. DISCIPLINE

We have already discussed what churches should be *saying* in general teaching. But there is another aspect to be considered, what they should be *doing* in specific cases.

'Discipline' used to be considered one of the essential marks of a true church, alongside preaching of the word and administration of the sacraments. This was applied from admission to exclusion (excommunication), with quite a lot (e.g. rebuke) in between. The church is a family, carrying the responsibility of disciplining its 'children', only possible where the 'parents' are disciplined themselves.

Very few churches exercise discipline over their members these days, especially in the 'Western' world. Many contemporary fellowships do not even have a recognised membership, so neither admit to nor exclude from it. The Lord's Supper is wide open to all and sundry. And an increasing number of believers don't want to be committed to the care of elders. It is all part of a wider individualism which regards religion as a personal and private matter. 'What right has anyone else to tell me what to do?'

The New Testament gives us guidance for our corporate as well as our individual life. Take the example of sexual misbehaviour at Corinth which was a public scandal reflecting on the church and the gospel it preached. A man was committing incest with his mother (or, just possibly, his stepmother). Paul would have acted himself, but faced the church with its own responsibility. And the whole church, not just the elders (a vital point to avoid tension between leaders and members). Paul told them what they ought to do 'when they were assembled in the name of the Lord Jesus', namely 'hand this man over to Satan, who could kill his body, ending his sinful life but saving his spirit from future judgement' (all discipline aims to be redemptive). All this is recorded in scripture for us (1 Corinthians 5:1-12), including more general directions about how a church should 'judge' believers who are sexually immoral, greedy, idolaters, slanderers, drunkards or swindlers. The others should not even associate with them, particularly over a meal. Quoting Deuteronomy (17:7; 19:9; 22:21, 24; 24:7), Paul says the fellowship must 'expel the wicked'. Quite a reduction for some churches! There is an interesting sequel in Corinth (2 Corinthians 2:5-11). The 'punished' member has come to his senses and repented. Paul tells them that though he was expelled by 'the majority' (it must have been put to the vote at a members-only meeting), they must all forgive him and welcome him back into fellowship.

How many churches today would follow these procedures? The author recalls a preaching visit to another country where he came across two churches with memberships counted by the thousand. The main pastor in one was on his third wife, after two divorces. The pastor and elders of the other were in the process of expelling a woman who was determined to divorce and remarry with no possible scriptural justification. Which do you think was causing the most gossip, leading to a public scandal which could damage the church's reputation? Yes, you are right. What a world we live in!

Ideally, the church should be involved from the beginning of things going wrong. Couples whose marriage is in difficulty need support and counsel, though this is not always welcome. When things have reached the point of considering divorce with a possible remarriage, the advice of elders and elderly in the fellowship is urgently required, but not often sought. When it is all a *fait accompli*, the church still has the responsibility to say and do something about it, but this is frequently avoided. In a secular age when religion is being privatised, the church is tempted to follow suit, its interference in domestic affairs resented.

It is precisely in matters like these that our corporate as well as our individual commitment to scripture is severely tested. And it has to be admitted that we are not coming out of it with flying colours. Maybe this volume will help us with future 'revision'.

I have only encountered church discipline on this matter at both ends of the ecclesiastical spectrum in this country, namely among 'Plymouth' Brethren and Roman Catholics (and the latter have qualified their position by the annulment of marriage vows in some circumstances). The Anglican compromise of refusing to marry divorcees but blessing their marriage after it has happened seems to an observer the height of contradiction, if not hypocrisy, but soothes the consciences of both the clergy and couple involved.

Part of the problem is the lack of a corporate male eldership in many churches. If one person tries to raise a standard he will draw all opposition to himself. But the root problem is the lack of courage to say 'No', which springs from a greater fear of man than of God and a reluctance to rebuke. When a church is struggling to survive, the prospect of losing disgruntled members becomes a threat.

However, a church that lowers its standards to keep people merely encourages undisciplined members to lower their own, in belief and behaviour. Christ's method was the exact opposite – he lifted people to meet his high and holy standards. We are called to do the same.

Author's footnote

This chapter is based on the assumption that readers already shared my conviction (that 'fornication' refers to premarital promiscuity disclosed or discovered *at* the time of the marriage) or have come to agree with me as a result of my presentation. In this case Jesus' exception is comparatively rare outside Jewish circles, which means that almost all divorces and remarriages today are illegitimate in the sight of God and my counsel is entirely appropriate.

However, I recognise that the majority of Bible commentators and translators, preachers and teachers, have held a contrary interpretation (that 'fornication' refers to persistent adultery *after* marriage). For this reason I respect their opinion, even while I cannot accept it. But I object to its use (abuse?) to turn the exception into the rule and insist that the utmost care be taken to make sure that this is the genuine reason, ground and basis of the divorce and not an excuse, a rationalisation. It will then apply to some divorces, but many, if not most, will still be illegitimate and to them this chapter must apply.

To complete the title of my book, remarriage is adultery unless one's spouse has died, in which case anyone is totally free to marry again and be blessed by God, the church and every Christian, provided it is to another Christian. That is my final word. The 'epilogue' is simply another event drawn from my experience.

Thank you for reading all of this book. May God bless you and guide you to your own convictions, for his name's sake. *Amen.*

EPILOGUE

'Mr Pawson, are you accusing us of living in sin?' The challenge came from a middle-aged couple, after I had preached in a packed theatre on a sweltering summer evening.

It had been an unusual meeting, the only one I remember when, while I was speaking, girls with trays had come down the aisles selling ice creams. I chided the congregation for worshipping at the feet of the goddess Isis! Then there had been a series of explosions outside, but in the absence of any warnings we had nobly carried on and only discovered afterwards that a nearby warehouse full of paint pots and drums had gone up in flames. The Spirit had led me to make a unique appeal at the end of my address: for *men* to come forward for healing. Many had done so.

Now this accusation brought me down to earth with a bump. As far as I can recall, the conversation continued like this. I told them I had never met them before, did not know them and was therefore not in a position to accuse them of anything, only to be told: 'But you said tonight that anybody who has been divorced and remarried is committing adultery and we've both been divorced and are now married to each other.' I have said things like that (and printed them, as you now know) but couldn't recall doing so on that occasion. Then I realised that I had read the whole of Luke 16, including verse 18, before I had spoken, so I said: 'That wasn't me speaking; I was reading what Jesus said.'

Then I opened my Bible and got the husband to read it to me. I have found this an effective way of diverting attention away from me, and my opinion, to where it should be for any Christian, on Christ and his teaching. When he had done that, I asked him how they thought they stood in relation to what he said, and he reluctantly admitted: 'I suppose we are living in sin, then.' Then he immediately tried to find excuses (reminding me of the man who 'wanted to justify himself', in Luke 10:29; don't we all?) The first was: 'It all happened before we became Christians.'

It is surprising that anyone should think sin is not serious when we don't realise what it is. But more likely he was thinking that (or had been told that?) at conversion all the past is forgiven and forgotten. Certainly, the penalty may have gone but consequences remain, like our marital state – single, married or divorced. I tried to explain all this but he quickly moved on to another tack: 'Didn't Jesus make any exceptions?' (had he heard this?)

I said: 'Yes, he did make one.' Again, I got him to read it aloud, from Matthew 19. After doing so, he was honest enough to confess that neither of them qualified. They had both divorced because they had fallen in love with each other and wanted to get married.

'So what do we do now?'

I told them Christians can discover that something which they had been doing was actually grieving the Lord and asked them what they thought should be done about it when they realise they have been sinning. Immediately came the reply, 'Ask for forgiveness.' 'Yes,' I said, 'that comes second, but something else is needed first.' They couldn't guess, so I told them: 'Repent'.

'What does that mean?' I told them it was not just saying or being sorry but putting right whatever can be put right, and asked them if they were ready to tell the Lord they were willing to do whatever he told them to do to put the situation right in his sight.

He looked anxious and asked: 'But will he let us stay together?'

I replied: 'That's for him to say, not me.' (I knew what I believed he would say to them, but I wanted them to hear it from him rather than me, not because I was reluctant to say it, but because I wanted to strengthen their relationship to him as their Lord.)

After a long pause, the response was frank: 'No, but will you pray for us?'

I said: 'I am very sorry, but this is a prayer you must pray for yourselves – and really mean it.'

At that point they left me and I have neither seen nor heard from them since. However, I met a man a week or two later who turned out to be the pastor of their fellowship and he greeted me with: 'David, you have no idea what you've done to my church,' which I confess put me on the defensive.

He told me that the couple who had been at the theatre on that Saturday evening had approached him before the service the following Sunday and asked if they could share something with the congregation. He told them they could have the pulpit and microphone after he had preached, assuming they wanted to testify to blessing received the evening before. He and the people were caught by surprise.

The husband said that neither he nor his wife had been able to sleep at all the previous night, and he told them why. They had been struggling with themselves over what they had been told. At dawn, they had knelt down together and told the Lord they were now willing to be obedient and do whatever he told them. 'But,' said the husband, 'it is difficult for us to hear what he is really saying because we so want him to tell us we can stay together. So would all of you, our brothers and sisters in Christ, please ask him on our behalf. And please don't be afraid to tell us whatever he tells you.'

'You wouldn't believe what happened then,' the pastor told me. 'All over the congregation the people burst into tears. Then confessions of wrong relationships and other sins were heard. Many were praying out loud. The service went on and on, but time didn't seem to matter. It's the nearest thing to revival we've ever seen.' I asked him if he was blaming me or thanking me for what happened. He said it was all a new experience for them and they were not sure how to handle it – but they were thanking the Lord for it all.

And now, dear reader, I am sure you want to know what the Lord told the couple they should do, especially if you picked this book up because you are in the same sort of situation as they were.

I don't know! I forgot to ask. I was simply grateful that I had played a part in bringing them to sincere repentance.

Thinking about it, I am rather glad I never knew. I don't need to keep it a secret, which wouldn't be easy. For telling you would give you a precedent to quote and follow, making it unnecessary for you to seek the Lord's face and will for you.

It would worry me if this book left you with no questions. I would be a substitute for your Lord and be guilty of encouraging you into that idolatry which the prophets also call adultery.

DID JESUS MAKE *ANY* 'EXCEPTION'?

Since my book was published, a reader has drawn my attention to the research of a Cambridge scholar, Dr Leslie McFall, whose 91 page paper *The Biblical Teaching on Divorce and Remarriage* can be downloaded from the internet. I wish I had known about this before I wrote. He reaches a similar conclusion (that Jesus banned all remarriage after divorce and even divorce itself), but by a different route. My case was based on the word 'fornication' whereas he had focused on the word 'except'.

Of course, no-one has the original Greek text of the New Testament. It has to be re-constructed from later handwritten copies of which there are now thousands. Dr McFall has pointed out that in the great majority of these Matthew 19:9 does not include the word 'except', only the phrase 'not over fornication'.

The word 'not' (Greek *mē*) is a particle of negation and would normally indicate an exclusion rather than an exception. In this case Jesus was contradicting the prominent Jewish teachers of his day, Rabbis Shammai and Hillel, who both allowed divorce for adultery (Hillel added other grounds). He was virtually saying: 'not even for fornication', even if that word is used to cover all sexual sin, including adultery.

This would explain the astonished response of the

disciples recorded in Matthew 19:10 (If there's no way out of marriage, better not get into it!) This surely indicates that Jesus was setting his own standard, different from and stricter than his contemporaries. It also explains why he went on to point out that celibacy is not an easy option, unless there is a reason or purpose behind it (verses 11-12).

It would also fit in with his repudiation of the law of Moses (in verse 8) which allowed divorce (Deuteronomy 24:1 and 3) and his reaffirmation of the law of God (in verses 4-6) which made marriage permanent and lifelong, with no exceptions (Genesis 2:24).

So how did the word 'except' get into Matthew 19:9 in almost all English versions of the last four hundred years?

The two-letter Greek word for 'not' is '*me*' but changes to 'except' when the word 'if' (Greek '*ei*' or '*ean*') is put in front of it ('*ei me*' or '*ean me*'). It is a tiny addition with radical results, changing an exclusion into an exception. And this change had been made in the Greek version of the New Testament used by all the Protestant Reformers and their successors, who accepted the alteration without question and incorporated it into their translations of the Bible.

Ironically, this text had been prepared and published by a Dutch Roman Catholic priest called Erasmus, in 1516, just in time for the Reformation, and beating the Roman Church's official Greek text in 1522. As a humanist, he had great sympathy for those who were finding marriage intolerable and found two 'loopholes' for them in the New Testament.

First, by adding the word 'except' to Matthew 19:9 he opened the door for both divorce and remarriage on the grounds of sexual infidelity, thus making Jesus agree with the rabbis of his day. Second, by applying 'not bound' in 1 Corinthians 7:15 to the bond of marriage rather than the bondage of slavery and to the future rather than the past (for a refutation of this dual error see Chapter 6 above), he was opening another door for divorce and remarriage on the ground of desertion by a non-Christian partner. To this day this is called 'the Erasmian exception'.

Both deviations from fifteen hundred years of church teaching and practice were seized upon by anti-Roman Protestant Reformers and enshrined in later statements of faith like the Westminster Confession. More importantly, they have been incorporated into most English translations of the Bible, from Tyndale (1525) onwards, with 'except' instead of 'not' in Matthew 19:9 and 'is not bound' instead of 'were not enslaved' in 1 Corinthians 7:15. The reader is invited to compare the New International Version with the United Bible Societies' and the Nestle-Aland Greek texts on which it was based. Any interlinear edition will reveal how post-Erasmian tradition has over-ridden the original text.

McFall adds the interesting information that we simply do not know whether rabbis Hillel and Shammai were contemporaries of Jesus. Retrospective references to them are found in the Talmud, which was compiled much later. Scholars have assumed that Jesus knew them because of the phrase 'for *any* cause', which was used by Hillel against Shammai's interpretation of 'indecent thing' in Deuteronomy 24:1 as 'adultery only'. But it is more likely that Jesus had his own independent view rather than that he lined up with either side of that rabbinical dispute.

It remains to add this author's opinion of McFall's case. In a word, I am not convinced. He is certainly correct in claiming that the vast majority of early Greek manuscripts of the New Testament do not contain the word 'except' in Matthew 19:9, and read simply 'not for fornication'. But whether the negative 'not' should be taken to mean 'if not' or 'not even' is, I believe, open to debate. The fact that Matthew 5:32 does have 'except' (or rather, the Greek is literally 'apart from') might support a similar meaning in 19:9; but could also indicate an adaptation of the latter text to conform to the former. Of one thing I am sure. To build one's view on such a vital issue on just one verse, and one whose meaning is somewhat ambiguous, would be a mistake. To put it another way, a verse that is in any way *obscure* should be weighed against others on the same subject that are quite *clear* (in this case, Mark 10:11–12; Luke 16:18).

With another of McFall's arguments I fully agree. He points to the scriptures which teach that if we are not willing to forgive others we cannot expect to be forgiven ourselves (Matthew 6:14–15; 18:23–35). This must surely apply when married spouses sin against each other, including adultery, though we must add the crucial phrase 'if he repents' (Luke 17:3). To be practical, separation may be the only possible solution in exceptional circumstances (for example, extreme abuse or cruelty), but to resort to divorce is to accuse a spouse of committing an unforgivable sin, either then or at any time in the future. The only such sin in scripture has nothing to do with sex or marriage (Matthew 12:32). Therefore to divorce one's partner is to put one's own forgiveness in jeopardy. For grace there is no such thing as an 'impossible' marriage. The door of repentance leading to reconciliation must always be kept open. Divorce and, even more, remarriage, close it. So Dr McFall and I are agreed that divorce and remarriage are contrary to the will of God, for believer and unbeliever alike, even though we have reached the same conclusion by different routes.

Books by David Pawson available from
www.davidpawsonbooks.com
A Commentary on the Gospel of **Mark**
A Commentary on the Gospel of **John**
A Commentary on **Romans**
A Commentary on **Galatians**
A Commentary on **Hebrews**
A Commentary on **Jude**
A Commentary on the Book of **Revelation**
By God, I Will (The Biblical Covenants)
Christianity Explained
Come with me through **Isaiah**
Defending Christian Zionism
Explaining the Resurrection
Explaining the Second Coming
Explaining Water Baptism
Is John 3:16 the Gospel?
Israel in the New Testament
Jesus Baptises in One Holy Spirit
JESUS: The Seven Wonders of HIStory
Leadership is Male
Living in Hope
Loose Leaves from My Bible
Not as Bad as the Truth (autobiography)
Once Saved, Always Saved?
Practising the Principles of Prayer
Remarriage is Adultery Unless ...
Simon Peter *The Reed and the Rock*
The Challenge of Islam to Christians
The God and the Gospel of Righteousness
The Maker's Instructions (A new look at the 10 Commandments)
The Normal Christian Birth
The Road to Hell
Unlocking the Bible
When Jesus Returns
Where has the Body been for 2000 years?
Where is Jesus Now?
Why Does God Allow Natural Disasters?
Word and Spirit Together

Unlocking the Bible
is also available in DVD format from
www.davidpawson.com

Made in the USA
Coppell, TX
01 August 2020

32190134R00075